Table of Contents

CTEL1

Pragmatics
social funct of language
Register

Phon
morphology
syntax
semantic

Krashen

ph sy

6:45
end @ 7:35

Practice Test #1

CTEL 1

1. Second-grade English language learners (ELLs) are struggling with pronunciation of an English-language phoneme not found in their native language. Of the following strategies, which would be the best step for their teacher to do first?
    a. Show them the phoneme's point of articulation on a model or diagram of the human mouth.
    b. Repeat the sound while pointing at its associated alphabet letter on a chart multiple times.
    c. Assign rhyming words in poems and songs as minimal pairs to place it in whole-word contexts.
    d. Read stories, paragraphs, and dialogues aloud, so they hear it in meaningful discourse contexts.

c

2. English language learner (ELL) students in an English language development (ELD) class at the early-advanced level typically show writing errors like the underlined part of the following: "We studied all week. To get good scores on the test." Which of the following should their teacher first instruct them to learn?
    a. Discriminating between infinitive phrases and prepositional phrases
    b. Discriminating between clauses as direct objects and indirect objects
    c. Discriminating between subordinating and coordinating conjunctions
    d. Discriminating between independent clauses and dependent clauses

d

3. Spanish-speaking students learning English commonly add /ɛ/ before word-initial consonant clusters like /sp/, /st/, /spr/, /str/, and so on, for example, "espeak," "estudy," "esprinkle," "estrike." Why does this happen?
    a. Their native language has no comparable such consonant clusters in it.
    b. Their native language always precedes consonant clusters with the /ɛ/.
    c. Their native language always separates these consonants with vowels.
    d. Their native language excludes one of the consonants in each cluster.

b

4. A Chinese student learning English tends to speak and write constructions like this: "This dish is my favorite because it has shrimp, snow pea, water chestnut, and bamboo shoot." To correct the errors represented in this sentence, what part of the English language does he teacher need to address?
    a. morphology
    b. phonology
    c. semantics
    d. syntax

a

5. A Mexican student is aghast when an American classmate tries to communicate with her in Spanish and translates *embarrassed* to *embarazada*. The teacher helps her explain to the American classmate that, in Spanish, this word means pregnant. What is this difference an example?
    a. Cognates
    b. False cognates
    c. Multiple meanings
    d. A syntactic mistake

b

- 1 -

Semantics = meaning
Syntax = arrangement of words

6. Since coming to America, Fredo has learned to speak English using different vocabulary words and sentence structures when addressing his teachers and principal than he does when conversing with his friends. This is an example of which of the following?
    a. The influence of contextual discourse factors on language variation choices
    b. The persistence of a native regional dialect's characteristics after relocating
    c. The differences between English language learner (ELL) students' correct and incorrect constructions
    d. The influence of an ELL student's native language on his speaking in English

7. A high school teacher wants to familiarize ELL students with standard discourse structures and conventions used in academic essays. Which activity would be most appropriate for this purpose?
    a. Assign small groups to brainstorm essay topics, write short drafts, and analyze these together.
    b. Give them copies of essays with key vocabulary words missing, and have them complete these.
    c. Have them analyze various essay types, and identify which vocabulary and grammar they share.
    d. Help them analyze provided sample essays, and make graphic organizers of various essay types.

8. Sylvia is a high school English language learner (EL)L student. When given oral discourse activities, she is very good at addressing points classmates have just brought up, organizing her ideas, unifying her overall message, and finding appropriate English words and phrases to make connections and transitions between sentences. However, she speaks very slowly, with many pauses and interruptions between phrases and sentences. On which area does she need to work?
    a. Responsivity
    b. Coherence
    c. Cohesion
    d. Fluency

9. An English language learner (ELL) student from Italy shows strengths in oral discourse, including good eye contact and expressive physical gestures. However, his American classmates are put off by his maintaining closer physical proximity than they expect when conversing with them. What is this cultural difference a feature of?
    a. Discourse in using language
    b. Semantics in using language
    c. Pragmatics in using language
    d. Social functions of language

10. Which of the following is a morphological feature?
    a. The combination of roots and affixes *morph*
    b. The patterns of intonation in speech
    c. The pitches of a voice during speech
    d. The relationship of letters to sounds *phonolgy*

11. Which of the following English words has a Greek origin?
    a. Calorie
    b. Calendar
    c. Calumny
    d. Calisthenics

-2-

12. Of the following words, which has roots in both Greek and Latin?
    a. Camera
    b. Calcium
    c. Campus
    d. Canister

13. Among the following pairs, which two words share the same root?
    a. Clinic and recline
    b. Clause and clavicle
    c. Clavicle and clavichord
    d. Iconoclast and claustrophobia

14. To promote English learners' language development, what does knowledge of morphology informing word analysis related to *solve, solvent, solution; absolve, absolute, absolution;* and *dissolve, dissolute, dissolution* most promote?
    a. Spelling
    b. Fluency.
    c. Vocabulary
    d. None of these

15. Why might Spanish-speaking English language learner (ELL) students fail to pronounce the initial letter *h* in English words?
    a. There is no such letter in their native language alphabet.
    b. There are no similar phonemes in their native language.
    c. The letter *h* when word-initial is always silent in Spanish.
    d. They are generalizing from some English silent-h words.

16. The California State Board of Education Adopted Reading Language Arts (RLA)/English Language Development (ELD) programs focus on the instructional needs of
    a. students learning English as a new language only.
    b. students learning English and those with disabilities.
    c. English language learner (ELL) students, disabled students, and struggling readers.
    d. all these and African American vernacular English students.

17. An English language learner (ELL) student writes this sentence: "Understanding spoken English and speaking in English is harder for me than reading and writing English." What is the error in this sentence?
    a. The word order
    b. The tense of the verb
    c. Subject–verb agreement
    d. None of these

18. An English language learner (ELL) student whose L1 is German has a habit of writing constructions like this: "Now to the class we are going." In which of the following does the teacher need to give the student more instruction?
    a. A larger English lexicon for more choice of vocabulary words
    b. The differing word orders used in English versus German syntax
    c. English verb tense conjugations versus German verb inflections
    d. The different English versus German present progressive tense

19. In a scoring rubric for grades kindergarten through Grade 12 Speaking accompanying the California English Language Development Tests (CELDTs), which of the following is a component earning a score of 4 in the 4-Picture Narrative question?
    a. The student's response shows control of basic grammatical structures.
    b. The student's vocabulary is generally adequate for performing the task.
    c. The student's pronunciation errors do not interfere with communication.
    d. The student's varied grammatical and syntactic structures have few errors.

20. An elementary English language learner (ELL) student has learned some English expressions from American classmates and demonstrates his learning by greeting the school principal, "Hey, man! What's up?" This child has not yet mastered which feature of pragmatics?
    a. Idiom
    b. Setting
    c. Register
    d. Purpose

21. English language learner (ELL) student Jose's teacher helps him build his English vocabulary by pointing out and listing Spanish–English cognates, showing him their identical or similar spelling and modeling and explaining their differences in pronunciation. What is this instructional strategy mostly an example of?
    a. Using student prior L1 knowledge
    b. Teaching students decoding skills
    c. Systematic instruction in phonics
    d. Applying word analysis methods

22. On the California English Language Development Tests (CELDTs), the Sentences item on the grades 9 through 12 Writing test has a drawing of a man and woman at an auto dealership, looking at a vehicle with a price sticker on its window. The accompanying prompt says, "Write a sentence that describes what is happening in the picture." Among the scoring criteria, a score of 0—No Communication includes a sample response: "Two people a truck from the dealer." A score of 1— Emerging Communication includes a sample response: "They looking a cor for buy." What is true of these sample errors?
    a. Both samples are missing a predicate.
    b. Both samples use the incorrect word order.
    c. Neither sample contains any misspelled words.
    d. One sample has missing and wrong prepositions.

23. Which of the following examples reflects a geographic influence on language variation?
    a. The separated parts of a city or country, for example, Berlin and Korea, developed different usages.
    b. A village isolated in a mountain valley retained Elizabethan English forms for centuries.
    c. Some African Americans use nonstandard English with unique idiomatic expressions.
    d. Some low-income families lacking formal education use ungrammatical constructions.

24. Regarding coherence and cohesion in written and oral discourse, which of these is true?
    a. Coherence and cohesion are different words with the same meanings.
    b. Coherence is an overall unity of organization; cohesion is more specific.
    c. Coherence is connecting sentences; cohesion involves topic sentences.
    d. Coherence uses pronouns and repetition; cohesion, thesis statements.

25. A female student from an Asian country habitually avoids eye contact when interacting with teachers and school administrators. How can school personnel best address her pragmatics needs to develop her sociolinguistic competence?
    a. Refuse to interact unless she makes eye contact to eliminate the old behavior and reward a new one.
    b. Acknowledge her cultural norm, and make her comfortable by avoiding all eye contact in interactions.
    c. Explain the importance of eye contact in the United States, and assign her to research and write an essay on it.
    d. Respect her cultural norm, make new norms explicit, and gently encourage eye contact without forcing it.

26. Which type of theory most attributes language acquisition to the influences of context, world knowledge, and motivation to achieve goals?
    a. Social Interactionist theory
    b. Behaviorist theory
    c. Cognitive theory
    d. Nativist theory

Review

27. According to cognitive developmental theory relative to language acquisition, learning and discussing definitions of vocabulary words like *free will*, *truth*, *beauty*, and love would be most developmentally appropriate to which age or grade levels?
    a. PreK to 2
    b. Grades 3 to 5
    c. Grades 6 to 8
    d. Grades 9 to 12

28. Anna, an English language learner (ELL) high school student from China, remarks, "I often forget to put –s on English plural noun—nouns! I think this is because we don't do that in my language." Which cognitive process does Anna's comment demonstrate?
    a. Memorization
    b. Categorization
    c. Generalization
    d. Metacognition

Metacognition = Thinking @ thinking   *Review*

29. Which of the following is accurate regarding comparisons of first- and second-language acquisition?
    a. Proficiency in L1 acquisition is constant across situations but varies by situation in L2 acquisition.
    b. While nearly everybody learns L1 naturally, not everybody learns L2, which often takes effort.
    c. Second-language learners have as many opportunities to practice with native speakers as in L1.
    d. Older second-language learners typically take longer for initial stages than younger L1 learners.

Krashen

30. According to Stephen Krashen's theory of second-language acquisition, which method is best?
    a. Letting students produce the L2 when they are ready
    b. Forcing early student production of the new language
    c. Correcting student production in the second language
    d. Extensive drilling and consciously using grammar rules

31. Regarding Krashen's Monitor hypothesis, which of the following personality traits is NOT associated with overusing learning as a monitor of L2 performance?
    a. Introversion
    b. Extroversion
    c. Doubtfulness
    d. Perfectionism

32. English language learner (ELL) student Chantal is very aware that, although her English fluency and academic language are excellent, she has yet to learn many social idioms. Realizing that this will take time and many conversations with native English speakers, she compensates meanwhile by routinely answering classmates and acquaintances' "How's it going?" greetings with either "It's a great day" or "Not bad"—the two responses she has learned thus far. What does her strategy best exemplify?
    a. Repetition
    b. Elaboration
    c. Self-monitoring
    d. Formulaic expressions

33. During a conversation with several native English-speaking classmates and friends, Rosa wants a vocabulary word she does not know to describe somebody. One friend speaks Spanish, Rosa's L1. Rosa asks her, *"¿Cómo se dice desdeñoso?"* ("How do you say *desdeñoso*?") The friend replies, "Hmm, supercilious." Thanking her, Rosa continues, "He was so supercilious!" Of which L2 development strategy is this an example?
    a. Requests for clarification
    b. Appeals for assistance
    c. Code-switching
    d. Role-playing

34. Which of the following is the best example of how productive skills are facilitated by the development of receptive skills?
    a. An English language learner (ELL) student who understands more of what native English speakers say can speak English better.
    b. An ELL student who speaks English better is more able to understand what classmates say in English.
    c. An ELL student who can write English better is more able to comprehend what he or she reads in English.
    d. An ELL student who understands more spoken English that he or she hears has better reading comprehension.

produce   receptive
write   listen
talk

- 6 -

35. In a middle-school class of English language learner (ELL) students at the intermediate learning level, the teacher assigns oral reports. As each student presents a report, the teacher invites classmates to raise their hands if they need the presenter to explain or repeat anything they did not understand. How does this practice promote student communicative competence most?
   a. It helps them develop social language-learning strategies.
   b. It makes them more aware of grammatical components.
   c. It keeps learning in the Zone of Proximal Development.
   d. It applies cognitive processes to internalize language.

36. On the California English Language Development Tests (CELDTs), if an English language learner (ELL) student's response to the Sentences item in the Grades 2 to 12 Writing test lacks a subject or a predicate, and its content is unrelated to the prompt, which score would it be given?
   a. 2—Basic Communication
   b. 1—Emerging Communication
   c. 0—No Communication
   d. 3—Fully Competent Communication

37. According to research findings, which of these is true about second-language development?
   a. Students lacking previous L1 formal education take longer to develop social language in L2.
   b. Students lacking previous L1 formal education take longer to develop L2 academic language.
   c. Students transferring L1 features to the L2 always demonstrate negative language transfer.
   d. Students transferring L1 features to the L2 always demonstrate positive language transfer.

38. For Grade 8 early-intermediate English language learner (ELL) students, which classroom activity would give them the best opportunities to receive comprehensible English input and produce comprehensible English output in purposeful, meaningful contexts?
   a. The teacher introduces a new grammatical construction, gives explanation and examples to students, and has them paraphrase it and then find incorrect examples in brief text portions.
   b. The teacher plays a video on a social studies topic, summarizes the video orally, and assigns students to write down new vocabulary words from the video in personal dictionaries.
   c. The teacher has students read explanations of the phonological production of certain English sounds, plays them a recording of those phonemes, and has students practice them.
   d. The teacher demonstrates a simple chemistry experiment, assigns students to pairs to try it themselves, and then assigns them to small groups to discuss their experiences.

39. According to his Affective Filter hypothesis, which affective factors does Stephen Krashen need to be high and low to allow successful second-language acquisition?
   a. High motivation, self-image, confidence; low anxiety, affective filter
   b. High affective filter, motivation, self-image, confidence; low anxiety
   c. Low affective filter; high anxiety, motivation, self-image, confidence
   d. Low motivation, self-image, confidence; high anxiety, affective filter

40. How would frequent multicultural activities and events in a school tend to affect its English language learner (ELL) students?
   a. These would inform ELL students about education and career opportunities.
   b. These would help ELL students learn English by enhancing their self-images.
   c. These would exacerbate cultural discord among the school's cultural groups.
   d. These would interfere with ELL students' process of acculturation to the United States.

41. English language learner (ELL) students may, like young children developing native English, apply a rule for regular verb conjugation to irregular verbs as well, for example, "goed" instead of "went" or "freezed" instead of "frozen." What is the term for the process that these errors demonstrate?
  a. Memorization
  b. Categorization
  c. Generalization
  d. Overgeneralization

42. A teacher gives instruction in English to English language learner (ELL) students who all speak the same native language and then clarifies it by translating it into the students' L1. What is this is an example of?
  a. Code-switching for topic switch function
  b. Code-switching for equivalence function
  c. Code-switching for an affective function
  d. Code-switching for a repetitive function

43. In Classroom A, the teacher has provided English language learner (ELL) students English vocabulary lists and L1 translations of selected words and assigned them to write paragraphs in their L1 and then translate them into written English. In Classroom B, the teacher has provided the same materials but has assigned ELL students to small groups to collaborate orally on constructing paragraphs, writing them down, taking turns reading them aloud, and participating in whole-class discussion of the results. Both teachers give oral instruction, guidance, and answer students' questions. Which of the following reflects the pedagogical implications of each classroom activity?
  a. In Classrooms A and B, the teachers access prior knowledge, scaffold language tasks, give comprehensible input and output opportunities, and promote communicative classroom interactions.
  b. In Classroom A, the teacher accesses prior knowledge and scaffolds language tasks but does not provide comprehensible input and output opportunities or promote communicative interactions.
  c. In Classroom B, the teacher provides comprehensible input and output opportunities and promotes communicative classroom interactions but does not access prior knowledge or scaffold language tasks.
  d. In Classroom B, the teacher accesses prior knowledge and scaffolds language tasks but does not provide comprehensible input and output opportunities or promote communicative interactions.

44. An English language learner (ELL) student has learned the –ed ending rule for past tense and past perfect tense with regular English verbs, for example, *look, looked, have* or *has looked* or *stay, stayed,* or *have* or *has stayed,* and so on. Now, additionally, she determines that certain irregular English verbs share common vowel changes, for example, *speak, spoke, spoken; freeze, froze, frozen; awake, awoke, awoken,* and so on. In which cognitive process is the student engaging by observing and differentiating these two rules?
  a. Memorization
  b. Generalization
  c. Categorization
  d. Overgeneralization

- 8 -

45. For which of the following vocabulary tasks would an English language learner (ELL) student most likely apply the cognitive strategy of memorization?
    a. Enlarging his or her lexicon of English vocabulary words
    b. Distinguishing among nouns, verbs, adjectives, and adverbs
    c. Understanding *–tion* makes Latin-root verbs into nouns
    d. Remembering words starting with *ps-*come from Greek

46. The California English Language Development Tests (CELDTs) describe certain kindergarten to Grade 1 students as beginning "to combine . . . elements of . . . English in complex, cognitively demanding situations and are able to use English . . . for learning in academic domains. They are able to identify and summarize most concrete details and abstract concepts during unmodified instruction in most academic domains." This is part of the performance descriptor for which level of English language development? *(Review)*
    a. Advanced
    b. Intermediate
    c. Early Advanced
    d. Early Intermediate

47. An Iranian English language learner (ELL) student relocated to Atlanta, Georgia, is trying to relate an enjoyable recent tourism experience to a classmate. Groping for the name of the place, he says, "Plantation." The classmate, assuming he visited an area antebellum plantation preserved as an historical attraction, responds, "You mean Stately Oaks in Jonesboro?" The ELL student replies, "No, it was . . . so beautiful, all the stars!" Instantly the classmate understands: "Oh, you mean the planetarium!" The ELL student confirms, "Yes! Planetarium!" (There are four planetaria in Iran, whereas many more U.S. cities have them.) In correcting his own word substitution and the classmate's misunderstanding, which cognitive strategy did the ELL student use? *Elaboration Review*
    a. Repetition
    b. Elaboration
    c. Code-switching
    d. Self-monitoring

48. Assuming he or she can understand and speak some English, an English language learner (ELL) student taking a biology course for the first time is likely to need which form of English more? *(?)*
    a. Basic Interpersonal Communication Skills (BICS)
    b. Cognitive Academic Language Proficiency (CALP)
    c. Both
    d. Neither

49. A teacher has a new English language learner (ELL) student in her class at the beginning of the school year. The student understands and speaks some English, but this is his first American school enrollment, and there are no relevant previous school records. What is the first thing the teacher should do?
    a. Assess the student's language proficiency level
    b. Assess the student's previous knowledge in L1
    c. Give the student scaffolding for language tasks
    d. Monitor the student's English language progress

50. Among English language learners (ELLs), which students must deal with both a different alphabet and different directionality in English orthography?
   a. Speakers of Slavic languages
   b. Speakers of Asian languages
   c. Speakers of Semitic languages
   d. Speakers of both (B) and (C)

Constructed Response

In a written response:

Describe one contemporary theory of language acquisition.
Describe one method to teach English language learner (ELL) students aligning with the language acquisition theory you described.
Explain how this method is compatible with the theory you described.
Explain how this method would promote English language development for ELL students.

CTEL 2

1. A teacher plans a lesson for a third-grade class including early-advanced English language learners (ELLs): She will read a story aloud, then lead a whole-class discussion with students sharing their own experiences similar to those in the story, and then have them write brief narrative passages about these experiences to meet the California English Language Arts standard for describing an experience by writing a short narrative. Which would the ELL students in the class MOST likely need to complete these activities?
   a. Picture drawing substituted for writing the narratives
   b. Writing models and questions for guiding composition
   c. Paired oral practice before whole-class oral narratives
   d. Copying the read-aloud text instead of the writing task

2. In Wiggins and McTighe's backward design for designing instruction and assessment, in which stage are students expected to understand the big ideas (major concepts) in the unit being planned?
   a. Stage 1
   b. Stage 2
   c. Stage 3
   d. Stage 4

3. In differentiating instruction for students with special educational needs, which of the following reflects the manipulation of pacing?
   a. Covering the same content over twice the duration for greater reinforcement of difficult concepts
   b. Covering the same content over twice the duration to investigate some concepts more thoroughly
   c. Covering the same content by introducing new and unfamiliar instructional materials to address it
   d. Covering the same content by enriching instruction enabling cross-curriculum student connections

4. Which of the following is MOST accurate regarding English language arts (ELA) standards versus English language development (ELD) standards?

    a. ELA standards are only for native English speakers; ELD standards are for English language learner (ELL) students.

    b. ELA standards and ELD standards are both grouped into grades kindergarten through Grade 2, Grades 3 through 5, Grades 6 through 8, and Grades 9 through 12.

    c. ELD standards are pathways to scaffold and assess ELA standards acquisition by ELLs.

    d. ELD standards provide teachers with a blueprint for planning the instruction of ELLs.

5. Among the following dimensions for differentiating instruction, which is usually the one associated with the teaching strategies MOST frequently used?

    a. Complexity

    b. Novelty

    c. Depth

    d. Pacing

6. In English language development (ELD) programs, what is the main purpose of classroom assessment relative to planning instruction?

    a. Evaluating whether the school has satisfied all its program objectives for ELD

    b. Evaluating student performance and needs relative to specific ELD standards

    c. Evaluating which ELD proficiency and grade levels match which ELD standards

    d. Evaluating what the cost-to-benefit ratio is of a specific ELD program's design

7. An English language development (ELD) test is given to English language learner (ELL) students to measure their fluency in speaking English. However, many of the words included in its samples for reading aloud are beyond the vocabulary development of the ELL students' proficiency levels. The unfamiliar words disrupt their fluency reading aloud. What is this assessment issue related MOST to?

    a. Test bias

    b. Test validity

    c. Test reliability

    d. Test conditions

8. On the California English Language Development Tests (CELDTs), which of the following English language development (ELD) standards is the basis for certain items labeled under the category of Word Analysis?

    a. Read simple vocabulary, phrases, and sentences independently.

    b. Use decoding skills to read more complex words independently.

    c. Recognize and name all uppercase and lowercase letters of the alphabet.

    d. When reading aloud in a group, point out basic text features, such as the title, table of contents, and chapter headings.

9. Regarding the California High School Exit Exam (CAHSEE), which of the following may local educational agencies (LEAs) do for seniors who have not passed either or both parts of the test?

    a. Provide supplemental instruction, which includes summer school

    b. Give intensive instruction up to a year after Grade 12 is completed

    c. Add instruction without using funds allocated for Grades 11 and 12

    d. Supply instruction without using funds allocated for adult students

10. On the California Standards Test (CST), which strand or reporting cluster has the largest number of questions?
    a. Literary Response and Analysis
    b. Reading Comprehension
    c. Written Conventions
    d. Writing Strategies

11. A teacher has a number of new English language learner (ELL) students in class at the beginning level of English language proficiency (ELP). As is normal, their receptive language skills are more developed than their expressive language skills. Which kinds of classroom assessments would be MOST appropriate to give them until they develop more ELP?
    a. Textbook assessments
    b. Curriculum-based assessments
    c. Performance-based assessments
    d. Written-response, teacher-made assessments

12. Among informal assessments of English language development (ELD) of English language learner (ELL) students at lower proficiency levels, which of the following formats typically would MOST enable them to demonstrate their English language knowledge?
    a. Listening to spoken teacher questions and responding by choosing among pictures
    b. Reading written teacher questions and responding by writing down their answers
    c. Listening to spoken teacher questions and responding by writing their answers
    d. Reading written teacher questions and responding by choosing from pictures

13. Among student performance differences unrelated to language development that can need referral or special attention, which of the following is MOST likely to involve curriculum acceleration or enrichment?
    a. Gifted and talented education (GATE) students
    b. Special education
    c. Student study team
    d. Intervention programs

14. If a student is identified with both English language learner (ELL) status and attention deficit disorder (ADD), which instructional responses are indicated?
    a. Extending the duration of lessons
    b. Reteaching specific language skills
    c. Reteaching specific subject content
    d. Both choices (B) and (C) but not (A)

15. If a teacher assesses advanced-level English language learner (ELL) high school students' writing tasks using holistic scoring, which of the following is a limitation of this method?
    a. Scoring procedures are complicated.
    b. Students do not get explicit feedback.
    c. The method is more time-consuming.
    d. Students get improvement guidance.

16. Of the following legislative and judicial foundations of education programs affecting English language learners (ELLs), which is or are MOST directly related to providing them with English language instruction?
   a. The Individuals with Disabilities Education Act (IDEA)
   b. (C) and (D)
   c. No Child Left Behind (NCLB), Title III
   d. *Lau v. Nichols*

17. In one school district, the majority of English language learner (ELL) students have consistently scored more than two standard deviations below the average of native English-speaking students on annual standardized tests for several consecutive years. School administration responds by placing ELL students together in classes with modified content instruction and more time spent on intensive English language instruction. This represents an effect of _____ on _____.
   a. achievement gap; segregation
   b. retention; promotion
   c. segregation; tracking
   d. achievement gap; retention

18. Among the following models of English language learner (ELL) programs in California, which are NOT considered alternative courses of study?
   a. Structured English Immersion (SEI) programs
   b. Transitional bilingual educational programs
   c. Heritage language educational programs
   d. Dual-language educational programs

19. Which statement is most accurate when comparing content-based English language development (ELD) to Specially Designed Academic Instruction in English (SDAIE)?
   a. Both content-based ELD and SDAIE place equal emphasis on academic content and ELD.
   b. SDAIE emphasizes developing English language proficiency (ELP) through instruction in content themes and concepts.
   c. Content-based ELD emphasizes developing content knowledge, with ELP a by-product.
   d. SDAIE emphasizes developing content knowledge, with ELP as an intended by-product.

20. In California, when do parents of English language learner (ELL) students need to obtain an exception waiver?
   a. To have their children placed in dual-language or two-way immersion programs
   b. To have their children placed into mainstream English language classrooms
   c. To have their children placed in either two-way or English mainstream settings
   d. To have their children placed in neither of these types of educational settings

21. For a high school biology class with English language learner (ELL) students at the advanced English learning proficiency (ELP) level, the teacher plans a Specially Designed Academic Instruction in English (SDAIE) lesson covering single-celled and multicellular organisms. Of the following, which activity would be best for promoting the students' development in English language and literacy?

    a. Assigning them to examine an amoeba and a fruit fly under a microscope and draw labeled diagrams

    b. Assigning them to observe differences in an amoeba and fruit fly, discuss, and summarize in an essay

    c. Assigning them to dissect an amoeba and a fruit fly and create charts identifying the features of each

    d. Assigning them to collect amoebas and various insects and list their characteristics in data table form

22. An English language learner (ELL) high school student successfully conducted many chemistry experiments in his home country. Despite limited English language proficiency (ELP), he now successfully conducts chemistry experiments in his American school. What is this is MOST specifically an example of?

    a. Education

    b. L1 literacy level

    c. Prior knowledge

    d. L1 literacy transfer

23. A high school geology class is studying a unit on plate tectonics. English language learner (ELL) students in the class whose English language development (ELD) is at the advanced level are LEAST likely to know which kinds of vocabulary words included in this subject?

    a. Tier 1 vocabulary words

    b. Tier 2 vocabulary words

    c. Tier 3 vocabulary words

    d. All of these

24. Which of the following is accurate regarding the Language Experience Approach?

    a. The students understand a provided text by using various approaches.

    b. The students generate the text themselves during the lesson process.

    c. The students compose individual texts by using their own experiences.

    d. The students collaborate to develop a text without teacher assistance.

25. Of the following scaffolding strategies for student interactions with texts, which one can be used before, during, and after reading?

    a. Annotating a text

    b. An anticipation guide

    c. A frame of reference

    d. A key concept synthesis

26. In differentiating instruction of a multidisciplinary thematic unit for ninth-grade English language learner (ELL) students, which of the following applies?

    a. ELLs should be grouped only homogeneously to encourage their using team behaviors.

    b. ELLs should be grouped only heterogeneously to encourage all students to participate.

    c. Teachers should read aloud portions of the texts they use in the unit to the entire class.

    d. Teachers should prevent or discourage the use of sticky notes and highlighting in text.

27. When planning Specially Designed Academic Instruction in English (SDAIE) for middle-school English language learner (ELL) students with intermediate-level English language proficiency (ELP), which teacher approach is most applicable?
    a. Integrating in every algebra lesson language objectives for content-specific structures and vocabulary
    b. Giving ELLs more access to algebra lessons through skills and concepts at lower developmental levels
    c. Putting off lessons involving more advanced algebra concepts until ELLs reach advanced receptive ELP
    d. Considering math subjects rely less on language than others, planning lessons with minimal linguistic use

28. Which of the following classroom techniques is MOST related to stimulating conversation?
    a. Arranging the physical classroom space so students can see, hear, and reach each other
    b. Using and displaying maps, artifacts, prints, puzzles, and similar content-related objects
    c. Displaying and using various printed materials in English and students' native languages
    d. Using all of these classroom techniques as they are equally related to stimulating conversation

29. To instruct English language learner (ELL) students in a cross-disciplinary unit that integrates math and English language development (ELD), which of the following approaches would be MOST effective?
    a. Using peer tutoring
    b. Using team teaching
    c. Using educational technologies
    d. Using bilingual paraprofessionals

30. Among groups of English language learner (ELL) students identified by the California Reading and Language Arts Framework, which group can sometimes benefit from recruiting their parents to support and reinforce their school learning in the home?
    a. The Special Group
    b. The Strategic Group
    c. The Intensive Group
    d. The Benchmark Group

31. Teacher 1 tells English language learner (ELL) students their learning objective is to use alliteration in a poem and defines alliteration for them. Then he gives them a poem to read that uses alliteration. Teacher 2 gives ELL students a poem to read and leads class discussion on the poem's relevance to them. Then she assigns them to small groups to analyze techniques whereby the poet created the effects they discussed. Once they discover alliteration, the teacher provides its name and definition. According to Cummins's quadrants, which of the following is correct? (Note: Both teachers ultimately have students write their own poems following these exercises. This step is not included in the answer choices.)
    a. Teacher 1 goes from quadrant A to B; teacher 2 goes from quadrant B to C.
    b. Teacher 1 goes from quadrant B to A; teacher 2 goes from quadrant C to B.
    c. Teacher 1 goes from quadrant C to B; teacher 2 goes from quadrant A to B.
    d. Teacher 1 goes from quadrant B to C; teacher 2 goes from quadrant B to A.

- 15 -

32. A teacher of English language learner (ELL) students modifies the language in a learning exercise without simplification. Which of the following could the teacher do within this definition?
   a. Repeat utterances.
   b. Use easier word choices.
   c. Speak or read aloud slower.
   d. Exaggerate syllables or use word stress.

33. The last sentence of a story has this line of dialogue, spoken between two married adults: "Come on, honey; let's go home." A student reading or hearing this story would demonstrate the inferential level of meaning by which of the following responses?
   a. The couple went home together.
   b. The story had a happy ending for them.
   c. The author wanted a happy end for readers.
   d. The readers will be more satisfied by this end.

34. A teacher with a mainstream English language classroom that includes English language learner (ELL) students as well as native English-speaking students always calls on the first student to raise a hand after he or she asks the class a question. An administrator observes the class and finds the ELL students never get to answer, although some of them do raise their hands. What instructional practice does the teacher need to change?
   a. Provide enough wait time.
   b. Frame questions appropriately.
   c. Vary the question types by need.
   d. Do all of these.

35. A Spanish-speaking English language learner (ELL) student has early-advanced English language proficiency (ELP) and good literacy in her L1 but never received formal instruction in grammar constructions or terminology in her home country. Encountering an English-language textbook assignment requiring a conditional-subjunctive sentence construction, she asks the teacher what this means. Using the cognates, *condicional* and *subjuntivo,* is not helpful. Instead, the teacher gives the student an example of a conditional-subjunctive sentence in Spanish. Upon reading it, the student understands what kind of sentence is needed for the English-language assignment. What kind of learning strategy has the teacher used?
   a. Metacognitive
   b. Metalinguistic
   c. Vocabulary
   d. Translation

36. When reading an English text, an English language learner (ELL) student recalls that the phrase *jump the gun* used in the text is an idiom meaning to take an action or draw a conclusion prematurely. The student has accessed which type of memory?
   a. Declarative memory
   b. Procedural memory
   c. Episodic memory
   d. All of these

37. A teacher provides kindergarten English language learner (ELL) students with artifacts, clothes, and other real objects from the students' native countries. The teacher also teaches the whole class the names and uses of these objects. What is this MOST apt to accomplish?
    a. Further students' understanding of U.S. challenges to various immigrant groups
    b. Interfere with students' acculturation to the United States by using objects from other cultures
    c. Interfere with students' English language development (ELD) in vocabulary by teaching them words from other languages
    d. Further students' ELD by stimulating conversations through interaction with known objects

38. A first-grade teacher has a tradition of telling students a story every year that includes a Thanksgiving celebration. This year, he has some English language learner (ELL) students from other countries for the first time. How can he best adapt his practice to include them?
    a. Eliminate the tradition and simply stop telling the story.
    b. Incorporate a holiday that some ELL students observe.
    c. Modify the story with a more universal family occasion.
    d. Continue the tradition, so ELLs learn the United States' culture.

39. A teacher has a class of English language learner (ELL) students. One group of these students never had any formal education in their home countries; the other group did. The teacher differentiates instruction to meet their differing _____ needs.
    a. cultural
    b. linguistic
    c. cognitive
    d. academic

40. Which of the following is a software program that would most benefit an English language learner (ELL) student for learning to speak English like a native?
    a. The English as a second language (ESL Jobs Forum)
    b. The Reading Plus system
    c. Rosetta Stone's software
    d. Software For Students' Easy Writer

41. For fifth-grade English language learner (ELL) students who are at the intermediate English language proficiency (ELP) level, a teacher needs to select printed instructional materials to use in a lesson about rock formation. Which of the following is the MOST appropriate way for the teacher to guide material selection?
    a. Choosing a fifth-grade text and adapting its syntax and vocabulary
    b. Substituting manipulatives and graphics for printed text materials
    c. Substituting a concise outline of key subject facts instead of texts
    d. Choosing a fourth- or third-grade text to match student ELP levels

42. One theoretical basis for recent (2014) English language learner (ELL) literacy approaches is the interactive reading model. Which of the following is true of this model?
    a. It emphasizes interpretation skills rather than decoding skills.
    b. It regards reading as proceeding from the parts to the whole.
    c. It regards reading as proceeding from the whole to the parts.
    d. It emphasizes that reading proceeds in both ways (B) and (C).

43. Recent studies find that, relative to English language and literacy development for adolescent English language learner (ELL) students who are refugees with little, interrupted, or no formal education, teaching early reading strategies
    a. is ineffective as it is developmentally inappropriate for their age levels.
    b. often enables them to advance by eight reading levels in one semester.
    c. enhances their reading fluency but does not improve their vocabularies.
    d. is not applicable because they have age-level print literacy skills in their L1s.

44. Regarding California's English language proficiency level descriptors (PLDs), which of the following is accurate?
    a. English language learner (ELL) students at the emerging level have not yet begun to use academic English language.
    b. ELL students at the expanding level can comprehend and produce highly technical texts.
    c. ELL students at the bridging level are the only ones able to participate fully at grade level.
    d. ELL students at all levels can participate fully in all content at grade level with scaffolding.

45. An English language learner (ELL) student reads a text on world history that lists events in chronological order beginning with the assassination of Archduke Ferdinand. The student comments that this assassination triggered a series of occurrences that culminated in World War I. Which process of reading comprehension has this student MOST demonstrated?
    a. Making inferences from reading text
    b. Identifying facts and opinions in text
    c. Identifying cause and effect in a text
    d. Relating one's experiences to a text

46. An English language learner (ELL) student has written a composition. Pursuant to teacher feedback, the student adds certain words and phrases to make clearer, more logical connections between some sentences and paragraphs and removes some language that adds words but not meaning. Which writing aspect of the writing process does this demonstrate?
    a. Organization
    b. Evaluation
    c. Revision
    d. Focus

47. An English language learner (ELL) student writes, "I just visited Washington dc for the frist time." In which English language convention does this sentence NOT contain an error?
    a. Spelling
    b. Grammar
    c. Punctuation
    d. Capitalization

48. When a teacher makes a lesson plan using Specially Designed Academic Instruction in English (SDAIE), which must he or she include?
    a. Learning objectives for English language literacy
    b. Learning objectives for academic English language
    c. Learning objectives for grade-level subject content
    d. Learning objectives for all of these

49. An English language learner (ELL) high school student had limited formal education and literacy in his L1, but he can relate personally to a school text about water wells because he had experience building wells in a refugee camp before coming to the United States. How can the teacher take advantage of this?
    a. Scaffolding student interactions with the text
    b. Accessing the student's previous knowledge
    c. Scaffolding the teacher–student interactions
    d. Strategies to create background knowledge

50. Among the following contextual supports, which would be MOST cognitively engaging for English language learner (ELL) students in Grades prekindergarten, kindergarten, and 1?
    a. Realia
    b. Manipulatives
    c. Focus questions
    d. (A) and (B) more than C

51. A teacher is planning a Specially Designed Academic Instruction in English (SDAIE) lesson to teach social studies content to English language learner (ELL) students and wants to promote their active use of language regarding the content they will be learning. Which of the following is true about this lesson?
    a. The teacher should not let students use their L1s as it will interfere with their L2.
    b. The teacher can assign cooperative learning tasks to promote active language use.
    c. The teacher can facilitate active language use by allowing students to use their L1s.
    d. The teacher should be able to promote active language use through (B) and (C).

52. Which of the following assignments incorporates all four Cs of creativity, critical thinking, collaboration, and communication throughout the entire activity?
    a. Having students independently plan and then execute their own projects to solve problems
    b. Having students in small groups plan problem-solving projects and execute them independently
    c. Having students in small groups plan and execute original problem-solving projects as a joint effort
    d. Having students independently plan and then execute original problem-solving projects together

53. When teaching English language learners (ELLs), which of the following would be the MOST effective scaffolding strategy for accessing prior knowledge to introduce new concepts and vocabulary words in English?
    a. Relate concepts and words to culturally familiar ideas and L1 words in comparison.
    b. Compare concepts to similar new ideas, and offer multiple English word synonyms.
    c. Provide multiple visual aids illustrating new concepts and English vocabulary words.
    d. Design a hands-on learning activity wherein students use new concepts and words.

54. A school district is issued textbooks for each content-area subject and grade that their state department of education has formally adopted. Most schools in the district have mainstream English language classes that include English language learner (ELL) students. Teachers can best address these students' needs relative to textbooks in content-area classes with which of the following?
    a. Give ELL students textbooks issued for lower grade levels in these content-area subjects.
    b. Give ELL students condensed or summarized booklets as substitutes for these textbooks.
    c. Give ELL students the same textbooks, and provide L1 translations of key terms as needed.
    d. Give ELL students visual graphic organizers and manipulative objects instead of textbooks.

55. Which of the following is the best example of a teacher question during a Specially Designed Academic Instruction in English (SDAIE) chemistry lesson to promote critical thinking skills?
    a. What are the names of all six of the noble gases?
    b. Of the gases we discussed, which ones are noble?
    c. Which of the gases we discussed are inert gases?
    d. Is it easy or hard to compound noble gases? Why?

56. Of the following statements, which is accurate regarding front-loading vocabulary for English language learners (ELLs)?
    a. Before assigning reading, teachers must first scan the text to identify problematic vocabulary.
    b. For comprehension, students need a working knowledge of 75% of the vocabulary in the text.
    c. Identifying their students' Lexile levels will not help teachers for front-loading text vocabulary.
    d. Identifying student Lexile levels is useful, but Lexile Analyzer does not help with specific texts.

57. A teacher instructs English language learner (ELL) students in different text genres. After they have demonstrated the ability to identify text samples correctly by genre, the teacher provides each student with text in one genre and gives them an assignment to transform it into another genre. What research evidence supports this instructional practice?
    a. None; the teacher is simply giving the students English writing practice.
    b. Explicit instruction in genres promotes improvement in ELL writing skills.
    c. Having students switch among genres does not help them focus on text.
    d. This instructional practice benefits ELLs but not native English speakers.

58. A teacher preparing Specially Designed Academic Instruction in English (SDAIE) lessons for English language learner (ELL) students mainstreamed in an English-language class is planning small-group collaborative work to discuss their analyses and interpretations of English literature texts. What is the best way to group students for this assignment?
    a. The ELL students should be grouped homogeneously to facilitate communication.
    b. The ELL and native English-speaking students should be grouped heterogeneously.
    c. The ELL students should be grouped heterogeneously but at least two per group.
    d. The ELL and native English-speaking students' grouping will not make a difference.

59. Which of the following is appropriate for teachers in giving instructional feedback to English language learners (ELLs)?
    a. They should include positive feedback as well as corrective feedback.
    b. They should confine feedback to correction to avoid confusing students.
    c. They should use feedback vocabulary above their level to motivate students.
    d. They should avoid relating feedback beyond specific subjects to ensure clarity.

60. Among long-term ELs, underschooled ELs, and Generation 1.5 ELs, which populations are more likely to share in common the total amount of time they have been educated in the United States by the time they are high school seniors?
    a. Long-term ELs and Generation 1.5 ELs
    b. Long-term ELs and underschooled ELs
    c. Underschooled and Generation 1.5 ELs
    d. All three of these

Constructed Response

1. In a written response, describe three ways to integrate and assess English language development (ELD) standards into subject-area instruction across the curriculum. Explain how each method would promote English language learner (ELL) students' development of both literacy in English and academic content knowledge.

2. Name three federal laws or Supreme Court decisions that affected English language learner (ELL) educational programs, and explain the impact of each upon such programs. Identify what each law or ruling requires educational agencies to do when implementing programs for ELL students.

CTEL 3

1. To apply research findings about how English language learner (ELL) students' school performance is influenced by cultural factors, which of the following teacher practices is MOST appropriate?
    a. Teachers respond to ELLs' culturally mediated learning approaches by modifying instruction.
    b. Teachers respond to ELL students by emphasizing language instruction over cultural factors.
    c. Teachers respond to ELLs by developing comprehensive curricula for U.S. cultural immersion.
    d. Teachers respond to cultural factors by grouping ELL students sharing cultural backgrounds.

2. Which of the following are internal elements or external elements of a culture?
    a. The language of a culture is an internal element.
    b. The structures of families are external elements.
    c. The gender roles in groups are internal elements.
    d. The social roles in cultures are external elements.

3. Regarding the history of education, which statement is MOST accurate?
    a. Prior to *Brown v. Board of Education,* classes within schools were racially segregated.
    b. Prior to *Brown v. Board of Education,* black students were excluded from white schools.
    c. Prior to *Brown v. Board of Education,* schools were "separate but equal" but not now.
    d. Prior to *Brown v. Board of Education,* American schools excluded immigrant students.

Expectatn
Resp
interactn
Tolerance
Parent

Factors that support cultural div.
+ student achievement

4. A teacher discovers that an English language learner (ELL) student reacts to certain commonly accepted American hand gestures as insulting and others as indicating different meanings. This is an example of student diversity related to which of these?
    a. Internal elements of culture yes
    b. External elements of culture
    c. Both of these
    d. Neither one

5. Which contemporary theory bases intergroup bias on a hypothesis of self-esteem?
    a. Social identity theory
    b. Social dominance theory
    c. Terror management theory
    d. Optimal distinctiveness theory

6. Among the following cultural contact processes, which is MOST associated with loss of one's native culture?
    a. Assimilation
    b. Biculturalism
    c. Acculturation
    d. Accommodation

7. When English language learner (ELL) students newly arrived from other countries undergo culture shock, in which stage do their parents usually first become alarmed about their children losing their native culture and language?
    a. Honeymoon stage
    b. Culture shock stage
    c. Integration stage
    d. Acceptance stage

8. Which of the following is accurate regarding social distance and psychological distance relative to English language learner (ELL) students?
    a. Social distance refers to a student's degree of comfort with learning a second language.
    b. Psychological distance is a student's degree of contact with a new language community.
    c. Psychological distance influences include attitude, integration, and cultural congruence.
    d. Social distance is influenced by dominance, enclosure, cohesiveness, residence length.

9. A teacher gives students an activity wherein students volunteer one at a time to leave the room and the rest group themselves according to some common characteristic (e.g., eye color, gender, height, nationality). The student who left returns and must guess in which group he or she belongs and state why. If incorrect he or she may not join and must guess again. With every new volunteer, the rest regroup by a different characteristic. Then the class discusses their experiences and feelings. This exercise is designed to help students focus on which of the following?
    a. Diversity
    b. Exclusion
    c. Prejudice
    d. Discrimination

10. An English language learner (ELL) student from an Asian country is in a class where the current assignment involves competing with classmates to see who can achieve the highest score in an academic game or contest. Instead of using her high intelligence and competence to defeat classmates, however, she uses it to help them succeed. What is the MOST likely cultural reason for her behavior?
    a. The ELL student, intimidated by being new to the country and school, wants to please peers.
    b. The ELL student, being new in the country, school, and class, is trying to make new friends.
    c. The ELL student was raised in a culture valuing group cooperation over individual competition.
    d. The ELL student feels inferior to classmates due to language barriers and is afraid to compete.

11. Of the following, which represents a major difference in immigration to America after 1965 versus from 1900 to 1965?
    a. Immigrants to America were more likely to arrive from small, rural villages in their nations.
    b. Immigrants to America were more likely to arrive as whole families rather than individuals.
    c. Immigrants to America were more likely to arrive from nations speaking similar languages.
    d. Immigrants to America were more likely to arrive on the U.S. East Coast than the West Coast.

12. Which of the following accurately represents a fact about recent immigration to California?
    a. In the 2000s, more immigrants have been coming to the United States than in earlier years.
    b. Among people immigrating to California, a larger proportion is children than adults.
    c. Of the immigrants to California, those with less education uniformly number more.
    d. Immigrants in California have lower wages than U.S.-born but higher employment.

13. Among contemporary causes of migration and immigration, which of the following types of causes is most likely to result in involuntary migration to the United States?
    a. Educational
    b. Economic
    c. Political
    d. Familial

14. According to research findings, which is true as English language learner ELL students shift from L1 to L2 use?
    a. L1 attrition is beneficial to ELL students for their L2 acquisition.
    b. L1 maintenance is important for developing L2 vocabulary.
    c. L1 maintenance promotes cognitive benefits, pride, and confidence.
    d. L1 attrition is not beneficial to ELLs, but (B) and (C) are correct.

15. When assessing English language learner (ELL) students in their L1s, which of the following is the MOST valid consideration?
    a. Standardized assessment instruments are equally easy to obtain in the L1s.
    b. Qualified practitioners to assess ELLs in their L1s are as available as in the L2.
    c. Students assessed in their L1s can be overidentified with disorders or delays.
    d. Students assessed in their L1s can be under-identified for disorders or delays.

16. When assessing the language abilities of an ELL child, which of the following would be considered significant, consistent exposure to English?
    a. Three or more days weekly of an English-language school, day care, or babysitter
    b. Being exposed to the English language incidentally from the television
    c. Exposure to the English language at different times in the community
    d. Having been exposed to English language that is spoken at home

17. Because of cultural differences in social space, a person from _____ is MOST likely to feel uncomfortable that a person from _____ is standing too close to him or her during a social interaction.
    a. Italy; England
    b. Norway; Brazil
    c. Bulgaria; Estonia
    d. Croatia; Vietnam

18. In intercultural communication, an American would speak more _____, using _____ voice; an Asian would find this style _____ and _____. The Asian would speak more _____, using _____ voice; the American would find this style _____ and _____.
    a. directly, active, shocking, embarrassing; indirectly, passive, dishonest, irresponsible
    b. indirectly, passive, irresponsible, disrespectful; holistically, active, low-context, rude
    c. honestly, passive, impulsive, high context; euphemistically, active, perplexing, odd
    d. warmly, active, irresponsible, collectivist; coldly, passive, insensitive, individualistic

19. Which of the following is an appropriate intercultural communication strategy?
    a. Using Americanized names to make newcomers feel welcome
    b. Using generalizations about cultural groups to know individuals
    c. Finding out which terms cultural groups accept and using them
    d. Maintaining the usual interpersonal space to show it is normal

20. Regarding cultural conflict prevention and resolution, which of the following is MOST true?
    a. It is better to follow the Golden Rule.
    b. It is better to apply the Platinum Rule.
    c. It is better not to ask many questions.
    d. Diversity is among different cultures.

21. A classroom teacher is expecting a new English language learner ELL student recently arrived from a strongly collectivist culture. Which of the following first lesson activities is MOST likely to be culturally congruent for this student?
    a. An English literary interpretation
    b. A whole-class academic contest
    c. An independent study exercise
    d. A collaborative learning project

22. A teacher, observing a new English language learner (ELL) student's aversion to making an oral presentation before the class is trying to determine whether this is caused by a lack of confidence with the English language or lack of personal self-confidence. When she consults with a colleague whether to get the student coaching in EL speaking skills or individual counseling, the colleague suggests the student's attitude could be due to cultural values instead. Investigating, the teacher confirms this. Which factor MOST influenced the teacher's initial attribution of the student's attitude to linguistic or personal rather than cultural causes?
   a. The teacher's ignorance about the student's home culture
   b. The teacher's own cultural values, beliefs, and assumptions
   c. The teacher's own history of lacking confidence in childhood
   d. The teacher's lack of familiarity with the student as a person

23. A teacher wants to become more informed about how an individual English language learner (ELL) student's family applies native cultural traditions related to social occasions and interactions. If the teacher were to do only one of the following, which one would be MOST useful for this purpose?
   a. Informal conversation with classmates
   b. Interviews in this culture's community
   c. Home visits with this student's family
   d. Reading books on the family's culture

24. To produce a culturally responsive learning environment that accommodates students from diverse backgrounds, which practice by a school would work best?
   a. Grouping diverse students by background for content subjects and by English language proficiency (ELP) for English language development (ELD) classes
   b. Making homogeneous cooperative learning groups based on student background records
   c. Observing diverse students' approaches in various learning contexts to inform instruction
   d. Alternating heterogeneous and homogeneous student groupings for half of the day each

25. Which of the following is the OST appropriate teacher approach to support cultural diversity and student achievement equally?
   a. Communicating higher language expectations for native English speakers and lower ones for English language learners (ELLs)
   b. Communicating high expectations of all students, accommodating ELLs culturally and linguistically
   c. Communicating overall lower expectations for all students as a means of accommodating the ELLs
   d. Communicating high overall expectations of American students and lower overall of ELL students

26. Of the following teacher practices, which MOST demonstrates respect for student cultural and linguistic diversity?
   a. The teacher consistently corrects English language learner (ELL) students using L1s by telling them to use English.
   b. The teacher uses extinction with L1 use by not responding unless students use the L2.
   c. The teacher instructs ELL students to replace cultural tradition with American practices.
   d. The teacher shows interest in ELL students' L1s and allows and affirms their use of L1s.

27. Among the following choices, which is MOST advisable for providing a culturally inclusive learning environment in schools?

    a. Assigning homogeneous group learning activities, so students with similar backgrounds interact

    b. Assigning independent learning activities to prevent cultural conflicts during student interaction

    c. Assigning cooperative group learning activities for students of different backgrounds to interact

    d. Assigning students to the same pairs, so every partner gets exposure to a different background

28. Which of these MOST accurately differentiates characteristics of prejudice versus discrimination?

    a. Prejudice involves uninformed opinions, while discrimination involves unfair treatment.

    b. Prejudice involves the actions one takes, while discrimination involves what one thinks.

    c. Prejudice involves judging ahead of time, while discrimination involves fine distinctions.

    d. Prejudice involves exactly the same things that discrimination involves; they are equal.

29. Regarding some ways to involve English language learner (ELL) students' parents in the school, what is recommended?

    a. Back-to-school events for parents should be conducted using English.

    b. Organizing school orientation tours should include bilingual facilitators.

    c. Parents view informing them of learning opportunities as condescending.

    d. Immigrant parents have too much to cope with without volunteering.

30. For inclusive teaching, which of these would give diverse students more flexibility in instruction and assessment?

    a. Assigning every student a topic for completing projects

    b. Presenting information either orally or visually, not both

    c. Weighting all assignments toward final grades in advance

    d. Making some assignments individual, some collaborative

31. For making English language learner (ELL) students' parents feel welcome to become engaged with their children's learning, which knowledge would help educators plan how to reach out to them MOST?

    a. What educational experiences and backgrounds the parents have had

    b. In which language the parents are most comfortable communicating

    c. For how long of a time the parents have been living in the United States

    d. Which work histories and occupations the students' parents have had

32. If an educator does not know an English language learner (ELL) family's language, which strategy would help him or her learn from, communicate with, and involve them in their child's education best?

    a. Making use of structured interviews

    b. Making use of informal conversation

    c. Making use of community resources

    d. Making use of oral and written histories

33. In which areas is it appropriate for educators to involve members of the community in their schools and classrooms?
    a. They can offer their insights about various cultural traditions but not religious traditions.
    b. They can offer their insights about various linguistic traditions but not content expertise.
    c. They can offer their insights about various cultures and languages not content expertise.
    d. They can offer their insights about various cultures, languages, and content expertise.

34. In many public schools, what are the School Governance Councils composed of?
    a. School administrators, faculty, staff, and school team members
    b. School personnel members and members from the community
    c. School personnel, community members, and students' parents
    d. School personnel, community members, students, and parents

35. Related to culturally sensitive school conflict management, what is a basic conflict management principle?
    a. Conflict is not a necessary, normal, or natural occurrence.
    b. Each conflict style has advantages in particular situations.
    c. Certain conflict styles are never useful for any conditions.
    d. Conflict itself is destructive, but managing it is productive.

36. Among the following approaches to multicultural curriculum reform, which one uses the smallest amount of involvement in multicultural approaches to education?
    a. Social action approach
    b. Additive approach
    c. Contributions approach
    d. Transformation approach

37. Which of the following are included as guidelines for innovating and revising school curriculum to be multicultural?
    a. Countries and cultures of origin
    b. Not histories of oppression
    c. Implementers but not autobiography
    d. Local responses, not global inclusions

38. To make multicultural instruction locally responsive, which of the following is applicable?
    a. Educators should share international experience in only general terms.
    b. Educators should not ask students to share any personal perspectives.
    c. Educators should share personal information relevant to class content.
    d. Educators should incorporate student autobiographies, not their own.

39. When a teacher has students from Asian, Latin American, and Native American cultures, which of the following student values can he or she expect to encounter?
    a. Conformity valued more than individuality
    b. Competition valued more than cooperation
    c. More student talk interacting with teachers
    d. More student participation in class formats

40. A Native American student arrives to school late several days because the family's truck broke down and he walked several miles to get there. Another time, he turns in a paper late because there was no electricity at home and he completed the assignment using a flashlight. Which teacher response would best apply knowledge of the student's experiences and be culturally responsive?
    a. Penalizing the student for tardiness to enforce rules consistently
    b. Grading the student based on classwork and assignment content
    c. Deducting credit for both tardy attendance and a late assignment
    d. Excusing the tardiness but taking points off the paper for lateness

Constructed-Response

Describe some cultural differences in how English language learners experience cultural contact in the educational contexts of student interactions and problem-solving and conflict-resolution processes. Describe an instructional approach to address these differences. Explain how this approach would be effective for addressing cultural differences.

Answers and Explanations

CTEL 1

1. C: Activities using minimal pairs, for example, bat and vat or lease and lace, help isolate the difference between two similar phonemes. Additionally, placing minimal pairs in meaningful contexts like poems or songs helps elementary school students at beginning English language learner (ELL) levels recognize, discriminate, and pronounce phonemes not found in their native language. Second graders will not understand articulation point (A). (B) is for phonics (sound–letter correspondence), not pronunciation. Discourse context (D) is a later step.

2. D: The students used a dependent clause as a separate sentence, but it should be part of the first sentence. It is not a sentence–independent clause because it has no subject or verb. It modifies the verb *studied* as a prepositional phrase; even an infinitive phrase (A) typically still would not be a complete sentence but a subject requiring an additional verb (e.g., "To get good grades is a worthy goal"). It is not an object, direct or indirect (B). As a prepositional phrase, it poses no issue with conjunctions, subordinating or coordinating (C).

3. B: Unlike English, Spanish always precedes these consonant clusters with /ɛ/, for example, *esperar* (to hope or await), *estudiar* (to study), *espresso, estrella* (star). The students are transferring this feature to English words with word-initial consonant clusters. These consonants do exist in their native language (A). Their native language does include these consonants in clusters, not separated by vowels (C). None of the consonants in these clusters is excluded their native language (D).

4. A: The student is omitting plural endings on nouns because the student's native language does not use a separate sound or letter to indicate plurality. The teacher needs to work with the student on English language morphology, like –s as a plural ending. Phonology (B) would pertain to correctly identifying and articulating the pronunciation of English language sounds. Semantics (C) would pertain to identifying and using English words with the correct meanings. Syntax (D) would pertain to identifying and using English sentences with the correct structure and word order.

5. B: This is an example of false cognates. Cognates (A) are words in different languages with the same origin and meaning, for example, English *dictionary* and Spanish *diccionario*. False cognates sound similar and may have the same origin but have different meanings as in the example given. This is not an example of multiple meanings (C) as *embarazada* is not used in Spanish to mean *embarrassed*; the Spanish word for *embarrassed* is *avergonzado*. The only other word for *pregnant*, *preñado*, refers only to animals, not people. This is an issue of semantics (word meanings), not syntax (D) or sentence structure or word order.

6. A: This is an example of how factors in the context of a discourse influence an individual's choices among variations within a language. Fredo varies the formality of his vocabulary and structural usages according to social distance that is, speaking more formally with adult authority figures and more informally with friends. This is not an example of regional dialect persistence (B): Fredo came to America from another country rather than relocating within America, and there is no mention of regional dialect. This is not Fredo's English language learner (ELL) status influencing his correct or correct English (C): Neither of the variations he uses with adults or friends is described as having incorrect constructions. Varying speech style according to the persons addressed is not influenced

by Fredo's native language (D): This commonly is done by speakers in English and other languages as a sociological phenomenon.

7. D: Academic essays include different text structures, for example, comparison–contrast, problem–solution, logical sequence, attributive, and so on. Giving English language learner (ELL) students examples of these and helping them analyze the essays will familiarize them with the organization, characteristics, and parts of different essay types; helping them make graphic organizers that visually illustrate the various essay types' structures will not only acquaint them with essay formats but will also give them tools they can refer to for writing their own essays. (A) would give writing practice but no exposure to existing academic essay types. (B) would give practice with vocabulary using contextual cues but no familiarity with academic essay text structures. (C) would help ELLs compare but not differentiate essay types.

8. D: Sylvia needs to work on her fluency in oral discourse. Fluency is speaking at an appropriate rate, smoothly, and without pauses or interruptions. Her responsiveness (A) is good: She addresses points classmates have just mentioned. Her coherence (B) is good: She organizes her ideas and unifies her overall message. Her cohesion (C) is good: She finds words and phrase to connect and transition between sentences.

9. C: Physical proximity is a feature of pragmatics, like eye contact, gestures, idiomatic expressions, use of various registers, and so on. Personal and social space and distance vary culturally. In Italy, people stand closer to others when speaking than they do in America; in England, they stand farther apart than they do in America, and so on. Physical proximity is not a feature of discourse (A), which involves coherence, cohesion, fluency, structure, and so on, in using language; or semantics (B), which involves the meanings of words and phrases; or social functions of language (D), which are to give information, convince others of an argument or viewpoint, control others' thinking or behavior, or amuse or entertain others.

10. A: How word roots and affixes (i.e., prefixes, infixes, and suffixes) are combined to create words in a language is a feature of morphology. Intonation patterns in speech (B), vocal pitch when speaking (C), and letter–sound relationships (D) or phonics are all phonological features.

11. D: *Calisthenics* has the Greek root *kalos,* meaning beautiful, or *kallos,* meaning beauty. (*Calligraphy* and *kaleidoscope* are from the same root.) *Calorie* (A) comes from the Latin *calor,* meaning heat (*caldron* is from the same source). Calendar (B) is from the Latin *calare,* meaning to call (*class, claim, conciliate, council,* and *nomenclature* are as well). *Calumny* (C) derives from the Latin *calumnia,* meaning trickery or slander, from *calvi,* meaning to trick or deceive (*cavil* and *challenge* are also from this root).

12. B: The word *calcium,* as well as the words *calcite, calculate, calculus, chalk,* and *recalcitrant,* has dual roots: the Latin *calx,* the genitive case of *calcis,* meaning lime, which originated from the Greek *khalix,* meaning limestone or pebble. While some English words developed directly from one or the other language, some came from Greek earlier and Latin later after the Romans conquered the Greeks during the reign of the Roman Empire and adapted some words from Greek to Latin; others like this one retained two distinct Greek and Latin source words concurrently. *Camera* (A) originally is a Latin word meaning vault. *Campus* (C) is also Latin, meaning field or level ground. Canister (D) derives from the Greek *kanna,* meaning reed or rod; *cane* and *canon* are also from this root.

13. C: *Clavicle,* meaning collarbone, and *clavichord,* a keyboard instrument preceding the piano, both derive from the Greek *kleis,* key, and *kleiein,* to close (these Greek words probably contributed to the later Latin *clavis* and New Latin *clavicula,* the more recent sources of clavicle). *Clinic* comes from the Greek *klinē,* bed, and *klinein,* to recline or lean; *recline* comes from the Latin *re* (back) + *clinare,* to bend (A). Note: The similar sounds and meanings of Greek *klinein* and Latin *clinare* seem to suggest the Latin was adapted from the Greek like many other roots; however, dictionaries give only the Latin root for the words *recline, decline,* and *incline* and only the Greek root for *clinic.* This is related to how the words first entered the English language. *Clause* (B) comes from Latin *clausus* and *claudere,* close or shut; *claustrophobia* (D) is from the same root. *Iconoclast* (D) is from the Greek *klastos,* meaning broken.

14. C: Vocabulary development is most promoted by word analysis informed by knowledge of morphology in this example: These words are all derived from the same Latin roots, *solver* and *solutus,* meaning to loosen or free and loosened, freed, or unbound. Knowing these two forms of the root, plus the Latin suffix *–tion,* denoting a noun, enables English language learners (ELLs) to expand their vocabulary of related words.

15. C: In Spanish, the letter *h* is silent in all words (including proper names) when it is at the beginning of the word (e.g., Hidalgo, *hacer* [to do or make], *hermosa* [beautiful], etc.) Hence, there is such a letter in the Spanish alphabet (A). There is a similar phoneme in Spanish (B): The letter *j* (and the letter *x* in some proper names and the letter *g* before the letters *e* and *i*) is pronounced /x/—not the same as /h/ because, whereas /h/ is a voiceless glottal fricative, /x/ is a voiceless velar fricative—but somewhat similar in that they are both devocalized fricatives. Some English words also have an initial silent h, like *honest, honor, heir, hour,* and so on. However, Spanish-speaking students are not generalizing from these words to all English words with initial h (D): They are transferring from the silent word-initial h rule in their native language, which is much more familiar to them than any specific English vocabulary words.

16. D: The California State Board of Education indicates that its Adopted Reading Language Arts (RLA)/English Language Development (ELD) programs focus on the instructional needs of all these groups: Students learning English as a new language (A), students with disabilities (B), students who struggle with reading (C), and students who speak African American vernacular English (D).

17. C: The error is in subject–verb agreement. The student has included two subjects, "understanding spoken English" and "speaking in English," so the verb should be the plural *are* rather than the singular *is.* There is nothing wrong with the word order (A) or the verb tense (B), only the number. Thus (D) is incorrect.

18. B: The student constructs English sentences this way because, in German, the student's L1, it is common to construct sentences with the verb at the end, whereas in English, the verb typically comes before any objects that it modifies (e.g., the indirect object "to the class"). The student has transferred German syntax to English. This example has nothing to do with a lack of vocabulary (A), English verb conjugations versus German verb inflections (C), or differences between languages in the present progressive tense (D), which does not exist in German (neither does the past progressive; time expressions, e.g., "at this time" or "at that time," and so on, are added).

19. D: The California English Language Development Tests (CELDTs) scoring rubric for the 4-Picture Narrative question on the kindergarten through Grade 12 Speaking test assigns a score of 2 to showing control of basic grammatical structures (A) but with numerous errors, some interfering with communication, along with other criteria. Vocabulary generally adequate for performing the

task (B), along with other criteria, is assigned a score of 3. Making some errors in pronunciation that do not interfere with communication (C) is also assigned a score of 3. Having an accent but using accurate pronunciation and varied grammatical and syntactical structures with few errors (D) that are minor, along with well-developed vocabulary, precise word choice, and a coherent and effective story explaining all four pictures with appropriate elaboration and more complex sentence structure constitute the criteria for a score of 4.

20. C: This child has not yet mastered the pragmatics feature of register: As dictated by social distance and norms, the expressions he learned from classmates are appropriate for informal use with fellow students but inappropriate for the more formal address required with an adult authority figure. While the expressions in the example are idiomatic (A), the student has indeed mastered them. Setting (B) is not the issue: Idioms are often used in school with classmates, just not with the principal. Purpose (D) is not involved: The student's purpose was to demonstrate his learning of American expressions, which he did; he just used the wrong register, which incorporates these idioms, to address the principal.

21. A: This is mostly an example of using the student's prior knowledge of his native language to promote English language development. The teacher points out and lists L1–L2 cognates, showing same and similar spellings and different pronunciations. The similarity of cognates reinforces Jose's ability to add new English vocabulary words through his familiarity with the Spanish versions of the same words. Explaining and modeling the pronunciation differences help him make adjustments for correctly articulating the English versions. This is not an example of teaching decoding skills (B) as the teacher is not showing him specifically how to associate English letters with English phonemes. It is not systematic phonics instruction (C) for the same reason. It is not applying word analysis (D) because they are not breaking the words down into their component parts or discussing their etymologies.

22. D: The second sample has a missing preposition ("looking [for]") and an incorrect preposition ("*for* buy" instead of "*to* buy"). This sample also misspells *car* as "cor" (C) and omits the necessary auxiliary verb ("They [are] looking"). Only the first sample is missing a predicate (A): Between "Two people" and "a truck," a necessary verb–verb phrase like *buy, are buying, will buy, want, seek, want to buy, look at, are looking at, look for,* or *are looking for* is omitted. Neither sample uses incorrect word order (B), only omitted or incorrect words.

23. B: Some American villages established in the 17th century by English settlers were surrounded by mountains and forests, making them difficult to access. Dwelling in such relative isolation, the inhabitants were found to have retained certain Elizabethan English speech forms for centuries thereafter. This example reflects a geographical influence on language variations. Example (A) reflects a political influence on language variations. Example (C) reflects a cultural influence on language variations. Example (D) reflects a social influence on language variations.

24. B: Coherence refers to how text is unified and organized overall by using devices like a thesis statement and topic sentences; cohesion refers more specifically to how sentences within a text are connected by using devices like reference, pronouns, repetition, and conjunctions. Hence, they do not mean the same thing (A). (C) and (D) both reverse the correct definitions.

25. D: School personnel should strike a balance between recognizing and respecting her cultural background, which informs her behavior, and making American cultural norms explicit while gently encouraging her adaptation to them without force or intimidation. Punishing the customary behavior she has learned throughout life (A) is unfair and not an appropriate application of

behavioral techniques. Neither is it appropriate or constructive at the other extreme to imitate her behavior in attempts to make her comfortable (B). While explaining the significance of eye contact in the United States—to demonstrate that one is paying attention, show engagement and interest, and connect personally with others—is indicated, assigning her to research and write an essay about it (C) is not: This part of the answer would constitute an unwarranted punitive measure.

26. A: Social Interactionist theory proposes that context, that is, surrounding environment and language used by people in it; world knowledge; and goals, motivating children to use linguistic utterances to attain them, influence language development. As its name indicates, this theory emphasizes social interactions in language acquisition. Behaviorist theory (B) emphasizes the environment's evoking certain responses in the individual through antecedents (preceding stimuli) and consequences (ensuing stimuli) to make a behavioral response more likely to occur and recur. Behaviorism applies these principles to verbal behaviors among all observable behaviors. Cognitive theory (C), like Piaget's theory of cognitive development, is constructivist, proposing individuals actively construct their learning and realities through interacting with and acting upon their environments. Piaget related language development to cognitive stages, each with new abilities developing. Nativist theory (D), like Chomsky's, says that people have innate language acquisition devices (LADs) and universal grammar, enabling rapid language acquisition and generation of endless linguistic combinations.

27. D: While these words do not seem long, complex, or difficult phonologically or morphologically, conceptually they are all abstract. According to cognitive developmental theory like Piaget's, children are not cognitively ready to understand or manipulate abstract concepts until preadolescence or adolescence, when they achieve formal operations. While young, preoperational children (A) have concepts of freedom, truth, beauty, and love, their perceptions of these are very simple, intuitive, and concrete, as evidenced by their definitions of them. Older elementary and middle school (B), (C) students are in concrete operations: They can follow logic as long as it concerns concrete objects or events. Only high school students will be able to discuss these concepts on abstract levels.

28. D: Anna's comment demonstrates the cognitive process of metacognition—thinking about thinking. By observing a morphological error pattern in her own use of English, and moreover identifying its origin as the lack of a comparable structure in her L1, she demonstrates her ability to think about and understand her own cognitive processes. Memorization (A) would be demonstrated by being able to retain and recall information. Categorization (B) would be demonstrated by being able to sort things or concepts into classes or groups, such as parts of speech, verb tenses, and so on. Generalization (C) would be demonstrated by applying a general rule to all or most specific instances, for example, regular verb tense endings or vowel changes in verb conjugations like swim, swam, and swum; drink, drank, and drunk, and so on.

29. B: Nearly everybody learns a first language naturally, but not everybody learns a second language; and doing so often takes conscious effort, whereas L1 acquisition in infancy and early childhood typically does not. Proficiency varies across situations in both L1s and L2s (A). L2 learners typically have far fewer opportunities to practice the language with native speakers than children learning their first languages, who usually have numerous, extensive daily opportunities for practicing, particularly with parents, other family members, and caregivers. Because L2 learners are typically older than L1 learners who are usually infants and children, L2 learners typically take shorter times, not longer, (D) before being able to form sentences. Babies and young children take several years listening to others' speech, babbling, and producing telegraphic utterances before forming sentences.

30. A: Krashen advocates letting students produce utterances in the new language when they are ready rather than forcing them to produce early (B), correcting their production (C), drilling extensively, or consciously applying grammar rules (D). He finds learning depends on meaningful interactions in the L2, wherein learners are more concerned with the content they hear and express than with the form of what they say.

31. B: Krashen correlates the personality characteristics of introversion (A), lack of self-confidence (C), and perfectionism (D) with overusing the conscious learning system as a monitor of L2 performance, and extroversion (B) with underusing learning as the monitor to plan, correct, and edit L2 speech. Learners described as optimal users of the monitor use it appropriately, neither too much nor too little.

32. D: This is an example of using formulaic expressions as a cognitive and social strategy in developing English as a second language (ESL). Chantal selects the most appropriate of two expressions she has learned, which can apply to every social situation wherein somebody greets her by asking how things are going or how she is doing (also formulaic expressions) until she can develop a repertoire with more variety. (Note: Even some native English speakers rely exclusively on one formula, e.g., the young man who owns a business and answers every "How are you?"-type query with his standard, "I'm so happy that I can't stand it.") Repetition (A) is a cognitive strategy English language learners (ELLs) use to help them memorize new vocabulary words or expressions. Elaboration (B) is a cognitive and social strategy whereby ELLs can more fully explain what they mean when listeners have not understood their initial word choice or sentence construction. Self-monitoring (C) is a strategy for adjusting one's L2 utterances to be clearer or more acceptable.

33. B: This is an example of appeals for assistance, that is, asking for help with L2 vocabulary. Requests for clarification (A) involve asking others to explain or elaborate something they said that the L2 learner did not understand. Code-switching (C) involves switching from the L2 to one's L1. Although Rosa did that in this example, she did it only to ask a Spanish-speaking native English speaker for assistance with an English word, and then, supplied with the needed translation, continued what she wanted to say in English. If she had simply said, "He was so . . . *desdeñoso!*" to the group, that would have been code-switching and less effective because the classmates and friends other than the Spanish-speaking one would not have understood the Spanish adjective as fully, even accompanied by nonverbal communication. Role-playing (D) is an activity used in some English as a second language (ESL) classes to help English language learner (ELL) students practice using English for various common functions, for example, checking into hotels, buying houses or cars, buying airline tickets, asking for directions, and so on.

34. A: Understanding what native speakers say in the L2 is an example of receptive language skills; speaking the L2 better is an example of productive or expressive language skills. (B) is an example of expressive language informing receptive language, the reverse of the way it typically works. (C) is also reversed: Writing is expressive or productive; reading is receptive. (D) is an example of one type of receptive skill (listening) informing another receptive skill (reading).

35. A: Social language-learning strategies include requesting clarification, repetition, or elaboration to enhance comprehension. In learning languages, students use these to make up for language deficits like unfamiliarity with certain linguistic structures or vocabulary words a speaker uses and to comprehend meanings in new or different contexts. The teacher's practice promotes the English language learner (ELL) students' development of social language-learning strategies. Directing them to request repetition or clarification does not specifically raise grammatical awareness (B) or

apply cognitive processes for internalizing language (D). The Zone of Proximal Development (C) is the area wherein students can accomplish learning tasks with assistance from one who knows more than they could independently. Because the presenters and listeners are all ELL students in the same class, none is assisting another; and listeners' requesting repetition or clarification does not imply any presenter necessarily knows more than any listener.

36. C: A sentence without a subject or predicate is grounds for a score of 0—No Communication. So are content unrelated to the prompt; nonmeaningful single words or simple phrases; meaning distorted by incorrect grammar or syntax, missing or incorrect articles, prepositions, possessives, or plural endings; severe vocabulary limitations (random words or no comprehension); spelling errors that impede understanding; and capitalization or punctuation errors affecting meaning. A score of 2—Basic Communication (A) would include subject and predicate in correct order, appropriate content, and other errors not interfering with meaning. A score of 1—Emerging Communication (B) would include a simple subject and simple predicate in correct order and content reasonably related to the prompt, but other errors may interfere with meaning. A score of 3—Fully Competent Communication (D) would include subject and predicate with some complexity; appropriate content; standard English; no errors in syntax, grammar, function words, or spelling; adequately specific vocabulary; and some punctuation, capitalization, and other minor errors.

37. B: Studies find that, when students have had no prior formal education in their native languages, they take longer to develop academic language in the L2 they learn. For example, it can take them 7 to 10 years to develop academic language proficiency in the L2 instead of 5 to 7 years if they have had previous formal schooling in their L1s. However, lack of formal education does not interfere as much with developing basic social communication skills in the L2 (A) because (1) primarily, these are less demanding cognitively; (2) students are more constantly exposed to social language in their everyday lives; and (3) students develop these skills of necessity for everyday interactions. When students transfer features of their L1s to the L2, some features are incompatible and constitute negative transfer, (C) while others are compatible and constitute positive language transfer (D): Either or both can occur.

38. D: The chemistry experiment incorporates teacher demonstration, paired work, and small-group discussion, affording students many opportunities for receiving comprehensible input and producing comprehensible output in English in purposeful, meaningful contexts. (A) involves English input and output and paraphrase but not in such purposeful, meaningful contexts. (B) also lacks such purposeful, meaningful contexts and does not give students opportunities for producing comprehensible output that others can hear and respond to as (D) does. (C) lacks comprehensible input and output in meaningful contexts.

39. A: Krashen says that, when learners are highly motivated, have good self-images and high self-confidence and low levels of anxiety, then they are more able to succeed in learning a second language. However, when their self-image, motivation, and confidence are low and their anxiety is high, they tend to raise an affective filter, which functions as a mental block that interferes with L2 learning. High self-image, self-confidence, and motivation are equated with positive affect, which is a requisite along with additional elements required for second-language acquisition.

40. B: By hosting frequent multicultural activities and events, the school establishes a welcoming climate and shows its respect for students' diverse cultural backgrounds. A culturally inclusive school environment affirms students' cultural identities, enhancing their self-images and raising their self-esteem and well-being. This should make it easier for them to acquire English because

language and culture are so closely interrelated. Multicultural elements will not inform students about education and career opportunities (A).Including all cultures equally is unlikely to increase cultural discord (C). Acknowledging diverse cultural backgrounds is not found to prevent acculturation (D): To the contrary, research finds that, in America's melting pot, immigrants assimilate more easily into mainstream culture when they do not feel they must abandon or forget their original cultures but can retain and integrate them.

41. D: Memorization (A) by itself would not explain this process. While learners might memorize past tense or past perfect tense endings for regular verbs as –ed, applying the memorized morpheme to irregular verbs is itself not memorization. It does not reflect categorization (B) but rather a lack of it, for example, classifying verbs as regular or irregular and including irregular forms under the latter category. Generalization (C) involves correctly applying the regular verb ending to regular verbs. However, incorrectly applying regular verb endings to irregular verbs is an instance of overgeneralization (D), that it, extending the rule too far to include a category that should not be included.

42. D: According to English as a second language (ESL) scholars, English language learner (ELL) teachers and students may code-switch (switch from L2 to L1) for various reasons. When a teacher code-switches according to the discussion topic at the time, for example, during grammar instruction to explain or teach a specific grammatical point in students' L1, this has a topic switch function (A). Code-switching for an equivalence function (B) is not done by teachers, but ELL students not knowing the English word for something may give the equivalent word in their L1 to fill the gap and continue communicating. Teachers code-switch for an affective function (C), for example, to express feelings in students' L1 for establishing rapport and relationships. Teachers code-switch for a repetitive function (D) after giving ELL students instruction in English to clarify it by repeating it in the students' native language. (While this can enhance comprehension, it can have disadvantages [e.g., students' relying on the L1 translation, making less effort to understand English], so it should be used sparingly and judiciously.)

43. B: In both classrooms, both teachers access prior knowledge by providing students translated vocabulary words. In Classroom A, the teacher also does this by letting students write paragraphs in their L1 and then translate them into English. Both teachers scaffold language tasks by providing vocabulary lists and translations and giving oral instruction, guidance, and answers to student questions. In Classroom B, the teacher also provides opportunities for comprehensible input and output and promotes communicative classroom interactions by assigning students to small groups to construct paragraphs orally before writing them down and then switches to whole-class discussion of oral paragraph reading. In Classroom A, the teacher does not provide these opportunities.

44. C: The student is engaging in categorization by assigning different classes to (1) regular verbs that take the –ed ending for past and past perfect tenses and (2) certain (not all) irregular verbs that undergo the same /i/, /o/, /o-ɛn/ vowel changes for these tenses. It is not memorization (A) because she is observing and classifying, but not memorizing, two groups of verb conjugation types. It is not generalization (B) because she differentiates between two classes of verb types with different conjugated forms. It would be generalization if she learned only the –ed rule for all regular verbs or learned only the vowel change rule for all included irregular verbs. It is not overgeneralization (D): If she misapplied the regular –ed ending to the irregular verbs that would be overgeneralization (also called overregularization when it involves applying regular verb endings to irregular verbs).

45. A: The most likely application of memorization related to vocabulary tasks is to add to one's knowledge of vocabulary words by simply memorizing new words. Distinguishing which parts of speech words are (B) involves categorization. Understanding that the suffix *–tion* converts Latin-root verbs into nouns (C) involves metacognition (for analyzing and understanding language structures and functions) and generalization (for perceiving the general rule of changing verbs to nouns via the *–tion* suffix). Remembering that words beginning with *ps–* come from Greek (D) also involves metacognition and generalization.

46. C: This is part of the California English Language Development Tests' (CELDTs') kindergarten through Grade 1 (K–1) performance descriptor for the Early Advanced level of English language development. The K–1 performance descriptors for the advanced (A) level includes "orally" identifying "concrete details and abstract concepts during unmodified instruction in all academic domains," without "most" modifying details and concepts. It does not describe beginning to combine elements; Advanced K–1 students "communicate effectively with various audiences on a wide range of familiar and new topics to meet social and learning demands." The Intermediate (B) kindergarten through Grade 2 descriptor says they "begin to tailor . . . English language skills to meet communication and learning demands with increasing accuracy." They can identify and understand "more concrete details and some abstract concepts during unmodified instruction"— *not* specifying "in most academic domains." The Early Intermediate (D) descriptor says students "continue to develop receptive and productive English skills" and "are able to identify and understand more concrete details during unmodified instruction." Here, abstract concepts are excluded as well as most academic domains.

47. B: The English language learner (ELL) student used elaboration to correct his word substitution error and the classmate's resulting misunderstanding. Using only a few words, but focusing on the key word *stars*, he gave the classmate enough information, combined with the similar sounds of the two words and the classmate's familiarity with local tourist attractions, for the classmate to infer he meant *planetarium* rather than *plantation.* He did not use repetition (A); repeating the same incorrect word would not have helped the way that elaborating with different words did. He did not use code-switching (C); for example, he did not say the Farsi سـراهانیک، نمـا افـلاک for *planetarium.* He did not use self-monitoring (D) by reviewing the word he used and correcting it; he gave the classmate more explanatory information (elaborated).

48. B: An English language learner (ELL) student would need Basic Interpersonal Communication Skills (BICS) (A) for having social conversations and accomplishing everyday communicative goals with native English speakers. An ELL student taking a biology course for the first time needs Cognitive Academic Language Proficiency (CALP) (B) to understand and correctly use the technical terminology of the specific scientific discipline of biology more than BICS. While the student would certainly need both (C) for a biology class that includes working with native English-speaking lab partners, giving oral presentations, and so on, ELL students typically acquire BICS much faster and sooner than they acquire CALP: Generally, they have mastered BICS within six months to two years of coming to America, whereas it can take 5 to 10 years to master CALP (c. 5–7 with prior L1 formal education and 7–10 without). Therefore, the student would need CALP more for a first-time biology course. Thus (D) is incorrect.

49. A: The first thing the teacher must do is to assess the student's language proficiency level. She cannot assume his proficiency is reflected by his understanding and speech of English because social English develops much sooner and more rapidly than academic language and will not help him succeed academically without academic English language proficiency. The teacher also must assess the student's proficiency level to know where to begin English language instruction.

Accessing the student's previous L1 knowledge (B), giving the student scaffolding for language tasks (C), and monitoring the student's English language progress (D) are all things the teacher can do during instruction after she assesses his level of English language proficiency, which will inform these practices.

50. D: Russian, Polish, Ukrainian, Bulgarian, Serbian, and many other (but not all) Slavic languages use variations of the Cyrillic alphabet, descended from the Greek alphabet. Its letters differ from those of the English alphabet, but the directionality is left-to-right horizontal as in English. Asian languages (B) use a completely different alphabet of ideograms rather than phonically based letters, plus a top-to-bottom vertical directionality. Semitic languages (C) like Hebrew and Arabic use different alphabets than English, plus a right-to-left horizontal directionality. Hence, (B) and (C) must contend with changes in both alphabet and directionality when learning English, whereas (A) must learn a different alphabet but with the same directionality.

CTEL 2

1. B: Early-advanced English language learners (ELLs) in third grade should be able to compose brief narratives rather than having to draw pictures (A) or copy the text that the teacher read aloud (D) instead, but they may need teacher scaffolding for writing their own compositions, like writing models and questions to guide the process. They should not find oral narratives as difficult as written composition, so practicing beforehand is not as important (C) as writing support.

2. A: In Stage 1—Desired Results of Backward Design, established goals, understandings of big ideas, and what students will know and be able to do are addressed. In Stage 2—Assessment Evidence (B), what kinds of performance tasks and criteria will be used to assess student performance of their understandings are addressed. In Stage 3—Learning Plan (C), what kinds of instruction and learning experiences will help students attain the learning outcomes desired are addressed. There is no Stage 4 (D) in Wiggins and McTighe's Backward Design model.

3. A: Four dimensions along which curriculum and instruction can be modified, for both challenged and advanced students are pacing, depth, complexity, and novelty. Taking twice as long to cover the same content while additionally reinforcing difficult concepts reflects differentiating instruction through pacing. Taking twice as long to cover the same content while investigating some concepts more thoroughly (B) reflects differentiation through depth. Covering the same content by introducing new and unfamiliar materials (C) reflects differentiation through novelty. Covering the same content by enriching instruction and enabling students to make connections across the curriculum (D) not usually expected at their grade levels reflect differentiation through complexity.

4. C: Once English language arts (ELA) standards were established in California, educators realized many English language learner (ELL) students would not be able to meet those standards' rigorous benchmarks at grade level. Hence English language development (ELD) standards were developed to support (scaffold) and assess how ELL students were gradually acquiring the ELA standards. (A) is inaccurate because ELA standards are for all students, not only native English speakers. (B) is inaccurate because only ELD standards are grouped into Grades kindergarten through 2, 3 through 5, 6 through 8, and 9 through 12, in recognition that ELL students enter American schools at various ages, but not necessarily with English proficiency levels corresponding to the ELA standards for their grade levels. (D) is inaccurate because the ELD standards do not inform teachers how to plan ELL instruction. Hence, educators have developed lists of grammatical forms to teach

ELLs that match different English language proficiency (ELP) levels and prepare them for ELA requirements.

5. D: Pacing, that is, slowing down or speeding up instruction, is probably the dimension most frequently applied in teaching strategies for differentiating instruction because it is effective, inexpensive, and simple. Differentiating instruction via varying complexity (A) is effective but demands more teacher preparation and skill and appropriate learning materials to implement. For challenged students, it requires removing confusing elements, making lessons even more sequenced and organized, and focusing even more on major concepts. For advanced students, it requires enriching instruction, allowing students to work with cross-curricular connections or time periods or subjects usually not expected for their grade levels. Novelty (B) involves new, different learning materials, modalities, or methods requiring additional teacher or school resources. Depth (C) often involves advanced students studying the same content more thoroughly.

6. B: The primary reason for the classroom assessment portion of instructional planning in English language development (ELD) programs is for evaluating how students meet specific ELD standards and what they need to attain standards they do not meet. Classroom assessment is not primarily for testing whether the school meets all of its ELD program objectives (A), which is better done using accountability indicators; or matching student ELD proficiency levels and grade levels with certain ELD standards (C), which is typically already done by state ELD tests aligned with and referring to corresponding standards; or evaluating the cost-effectiveness of ELD program design (D), which is done outside the classroom by analyzing and comparing data such as accountability measures, budget analyses, and so on.

7. B: This assessment issue is related to test validity, which is whether a test measures what it claims or intends to measure. In this example, the test claimed or intended to measure the fluency of English language learner (ELL) students in speaking English, but using vocabulary words above their English language proficiency (ELP) levels interfered with measurement. Because the test was not designed to assess vocabulary, including words too difficult for the students' proficiency levels confounded the results. The question states this was an English language development (ELD) test, so it can be assumed the test was not biased (A) against ELLs or in favor of native English speakers but designed for ELL students. This is not an issue of reliability (C), which would emerge if the test got different results from the same students over repeated administrations. Test conditions (D) would involve things like noise, poor lighting, crowding, incorrect administration, inadequate pretest student sleep and nourishment, and so on.

8. C: This is the California English language development (ELD) standard that is the basis for one item under the California English Language Development Tests' (CELDTs') Word Analysis section of the Grades kindergarten through 1 Reading test. (Another is to recognize unfamiliar English phonemes.) (A) is the California ELD standard that is the basis for one of the Fluency and Vocabulary items on the kindergarten through Grade 1 Reading test. (B) is the California ELD standard that is the basis for another Fluency and Vocabulary item on the kindergarten through Grade 1 Reading test. (D) is the California ELD standard that is the basis for a Reading Comprehension item on the kindergarten through Grade 1 Reading test.

9. A: For seniors who have not yet passed either or both parts of the California High School Exit Exam (CAHSEE), California local education agencies (LEAs) can give them extra instruction, including summer school, corresponding to state content standards, to help them pass. They can also give these students intensive instruction for up to two years after they finish 12th grade, not one (B). LEAs can use funds allocated for intensive instruction for Grades 11 and 12 (C) and for

adult students (D) at their own discretion to provide this instruction to students to assist them in passing the CAHSEE.

10. D: The California Standards Test (CST) has 22 questions on Writing Strategies, 19 questions on Reading Comprehension (B), 17 questions on Literary Response and Analysis (A), and 9 questions on Written Conventions (C). It also has 8 questions on Word Analysis, for a total of 75 questions.

11. C: English language learner (ELL) students at the beginning level of English language proficiency (ELP) will understand more of what they hear and read in English (receptive) than what they can say or write in English (expressive). Thus, textbook assignments (A) will be difficult for them as these often will require them to write their responses in English, like teacher-made tests requiring written responses (D) will. Curriculum-based assessments (B) may or may not require spoken or written responses. However, performance-based assessments (C) will allow ELLs to demonstrate what they know and can do without having higher levels of proficiency in speaking and writing English.

12. A: At lower proficiency levels, second-language acquisition (like first-language acquisition) typically proceeds from receptive to expressive; that is, student listening and reading skills precede speaking and writing skills. Therefore, oral teacher questions will be easier for them to comprehend than written questions (B), (D), and responding will be easier by selecting the correct picture among several than by speaking or writing (B), (C), their answers. (Spoken responses would be easier than written ones; picture selection is easier than spoken responses.)

13. A: Gifted and talented education (GATE) students are most likely to need curriculum and assignments accelerated in pace or enriched in content to meet their needs, which are advanced intellectually or otherwise. Special education (B) students are more likely to need certain classroom accommodations or classroom or curriculum modifications to adapt instruction and assessment to their needs. Student study teams (SSTs) (C) generally determine whether a specific learning disability; medical condition; vision impairment; physical, psychological, or social problem; or other issues affecting performance cause students to struggle academically. (They also investigate language barriers, but in this case, the question specifies differences unrelated to language development.) Depending on their findings, SSTs recommend special education evaluation or other intervention programs (D).

14. D: Extending the duration of lessons (A) is not indicated for a student with an attention deficit disorder: This student would likely benefit from lessons of shorter duration, if anything (unless the teacher finds the student can succeed with lessons of the usual duration by using other strategies). However, with an attention deficit, the student will probably need the teacher to reteach both language skills (B) and subject content (C), which the student may not retain initially due to attentional limitations but may eventually retain with enough repetition.

15. B: Holistic scoring methods are less, not more, complicated (A) and take less, not more, time (C) to assess written compositions; these are not limitations but advantages of holistic scoring. A limitation of holistic scoring is that individual students do not receive explicit teacher feedback (B), so with this method, they do not get guidance about how to improve their writing (D).

16. B: The Individuals with Disabilities Education Act (IDEA) (A) guarantees students with disabilities a free, appropriate public education in the least-restrictive environment possible. Some students with disabilities are also English language learners (ELLs), so this legislation affects them. Title III of the No Child Left Behind (NCLB) Act (C) requires funding to be allocated specifically for

providing (English) language instruction to limited English-proficient and immigrant students. The Supreme Court case of *Lau v. Nichols* (D) involved a number of Chinese students in a San Francisco school district, some of whom did not receive English-language instruction, giving their lawyer grounds to sue on the basis that they were denied their rights to education because they did not know English and were not given the English instruction needed to participate. Hence, (C) and (D) (= B) pertain most directly to providing ELLs English-language instruction.

17. A: This scenario represents an effect of an achievement gap upon segregation. The lower standardized scores of most English language learner (ELL) students represent an achievement gap; placing them in separate classes for differentiated content instruction and intensive English instruction represents segregation. The example does not include any mention of ELL students being retained (B) (D) or promoted (B). Segregation is akin to tracking (C). While ELL students often need differentiated content instruction and supplemental English-language instruction, federal legislation mandates that such instruction be inclusive, not segregated.

18. A: Structured English Immersion (SEI) programs are considered an improvement over submersion programs featuring sink-or-swim approaches requiring English language learner (ELL) students learn English without any real help or support. SEI programs feature intensive, direct English instruction and lesson planning emphasizing vocabulary building. Both intend ELLs to learn English as rapidly as possible for inclusion in mainstream English-language content classes. While many educators disapprove of them, SEI programs are not considered alternative courses of study. Transitional bilingual programs (B) instruct ELLs in both L1 and L2 to enable more gradual L1–L2 transitions. Heritage language programs (C) include community, kindergarten through Grade 12, and higher education. Varying in most aspects, including dual language versus immersion, heritage language programs teach students' native languages to prevent their loss in America. Some emphasize high educational standards as well as native languages, cultures, and traditions. Dual-language programs (D) feature ongoing bilingual instruction without phasing out student L1s.

19. D: Specially Designed Academic Instruction in English (SDAIE) puts more emphasis on developing knowledge in the academic content areas, while English language development (ELD) is a secondary goal. Content-based ELD does not do this (C). Content-based ELD places more emphasis on ELD but accomplishes this through instruction in academic content themes and concepts. SDAIE does not do this (B). Therefore, both types of instruction do not place equal emphasis on both academic content and ELD (A).

20. A: In California, parents must obtain a parental exception waiver to have their children placed in dual-language or two-way immersion or other alternative educational programs instead of in a sheltered English instruction (SEI) or mainstream English language classroom. However, if their children are placed in the SEI program and parents want their children moved to a mainstream English language classroom, they do not need a waiver (B); they can simply request this placement. Therefore, it is incorrect that they need a waiver for either (C) or neither (D) placement.

21. B: For high school English language learner (ELL) students at the advanced level of English language proficiency (ELP), an appropriate and effective lesson for promoting English language and literacy should enable them to perform relevant academic tasks, apply critical thinking skills, engage in discussion to convey and comprehend meaning, and develop their oral and written academic language skills. The lesson that requires observation, oral discussion, and written essay summary including comparison and contrast is an example of an effective Specially Designed Academic Instruction in English (SDAIE) lesson. The other choices do not involve oral discussion in English or written composition in English.

22. C: This is most specifically an example of the student's prior knowledge. While chemistry experiments in his home country were part of his education (A), education is less specific as a reason for his success with chemistry experiments in America than his prior knowledge. This is not an example of his L1 literacy level (B) or transfer of his L1 literacy (D) because the question never states that he succeeded specifically in listening, speaking, reading, or writing in English about the chemistry experiments—only in conducting them.

23. C: Tier 3 vocabulary words are domain-specific, low-frequency words specialized to a particular content area or field. In this case, they would include terms like *lithosphere, continental drift, tectonic plates, subduction zones, convergent, divergent, transform motion,* and so on. Tier 1 words (A) are common words known by native English-speaking children like *move, large, small, earth,* and so on. Beginning English language learners (ELLs) may not know these, but ELLs at the advanced English language development (ELD) level generally do. Tier 2 words (B) are high-frequency, cross-curricular, general academic vocabulary words used across different subjects and contexts. In the example given, they might include *spread, shift, heat transfer, material, suction, drag, oceanic, volcanic, density,* and so on. ELLs at the advanced level are likely to know these. However, both advanced ELLs and even native English-speaking students usually do not know specific Tier 3 words until they study the subject using that vocabulary. Therefore, (D) is incorrect.

24. B: In the Language Experience Approach, the students generate an original text rather than being provided with one (A). The students and teacher work together to produce the text based on an experience shared by the whole class, for example, an experiment, field trip, and so on; students do not compose individual texts about separate personal experiences (C). The students and teacher discuss the experience together; the teacher organizes and records student speech on the board; the class reads the text aloud and discusses it; the teacher calls for any student additions or corrections, marks text changes proposed by students, and suggests additional changes as needed. Hence, the students collaborate with the teacher, not without teacher assistance (D).

25. C: The scaffolding strategy of a frame of reference instructs students to think about what they know about a subject and how they know this information. Thinking about these things helps students learn how to create mental contexts, that is, frames of reference, for reading texts. This strategy can be used before, during, and after reading text. Annotating text (A) furthers active reading and critical thinking skills. While reading and making annotations, students can use various helpful acronyms to help them remember components of the writing craft. This strategy can be used during and after, but not before, reading. Anticipation guides (B) are used as pre-reading strategies to stimulate student thinking and discussion of concepts and ideas that they will discover in texts. Thus, they are used before, but not during or after, reading. Key concept synthesis (D) assists students in identifying a text's most significant ideas, stating these in their own words, and interconnecting them. It is used during and after, but not before, reading.

26. C: Reading aloud portions or chunks of the texts they are using for the unit to the entire class is a good strategy to differentiate instruction for the English language learner (ELL) students in the class while maintaining inclusive teaching. Differentiated instruction should include both homogeneous (A) and heterogeneous (B) grouping of ELL students—not only one or the other—to promote both team behaviors and participation by every student, respectively. Another differentiated instruction strategy to help ELL students is to use sticky notes, highlighting (D), and other ways of annotating the texts throughout to develop content-area vocabulary, teach more difficult words, encourage student inquiry and questioning, and enhance ELL student reading comprehension.

27. A: English language learners (ELLs) with intermediate English language proficiency (ELP) can be impeded seriously in learning subject content by unfamiliar, content-specific language structures and vocabulary, particularly equation and formula syntax and technical terminology in mathematics and science subjects. When planning Specially Designed Academic Instruction in English (SDAIE) for middle school ELLs at the intermediate level of ELP, the teacher can give them better access to algebra content by integrating language objectives for these specialized elements into every lesson. Restricting instruction to skills and concepts at lower developmental levels (B) is inappropriate as these do not match the students' developmental levels regardless of their ELP levels. Putting off advanced lessons until ELLs reach advanced receptive ELP (C) is both inappropriate and unrealistic as this could take too long for them to learn algebra at the right time; plus, individual student ELPs progress at varying rates. Lesson planning to avoid language just because math uses it less than other subjects (D) is also inappropriate for teaching SDAIE, which while emphasizing content learning, should still incorporate English language, as its name indicates.

28. B: By visibly placing and making regular use of content-related objects like maps, artifacts, prints, and puzzles, teachers provide stimuli to start conversations with and among students. By arranging the physical classroom space so students are accessible to each other (A), teachers establish a physical setting that supports student interactions in general—conversations, study collaborations, and other interactions. By displaying and using various printed materials in both English and the students' native languages (C), teachers provide students with a language-rich environment. Because each of these has the related but distinct specific effects described, (D) is incorrect.

29. B: Team teaching with a math teacher and an English language arts, English as a second language (ESL), or English language development (ELD) teacher would be most effective for instructing English language learner (ELL) students in a cross-disciplinary unit integrating math and ELD. Peer tutoring (A) is more applicable to, for example, having students with higher English language proficiency (ELP) levels in some or all areas tutor students with lower ELP levels in some or all areas but not to planning and teaching a unit integrating math and ELD instruction. Educational technologies (C) are effective for many purposes, for example, interactive lessons, independent study, multimedia presentations, homework assignments, researching and writing papers, and so on, and can be well used to supplement the unit described for all these activities and more; but for actually planning and teaching a unit integrating math and ELD to ELL students, teachers are needed. Bilingual paraprofessionals (D) are most helpful for bridging communication gaps with ELL students, providing additional one-to-one or small-group instructional support, informing teachers of linguistic differences, and so on, but they cannot necessarily plan and teach a cross-disciplinary unit.

30. D: According to the California Reading and Language Arts (RLA) Framework, teachers can sometimes ask certain parents of students in the Benchmark Group of English language learners (ELLs) to help their children at home to keep them from falling behind in school if they encounter minor or temporary difficulties. The authors recommend organizing teaching resources to facilitate parental learning support. There is no Special Group (A) identified in the framework, though it does offer guidelines following the other three group descriptions for planning instruction for all students to incorporate students with special instructional needs. The Strategic Group (B) is described as needing reteaching or other classroom assistance; possibly a student success team to identify suitable support; specific homework assignments; paired assignments; before-, and after-school, evening, and weekend study groups; extended study time blocks for English language development (ELD); specific classroom, curriculum, or instruction accommodations or

modifications, including for students with disabilities; and Individualized education plans (IEPs) for students with disabilities. The Intensive Group (C) is described as needing referral to a student success team to discuss options and possibly to special education services including intensive specialist intervention; specialized equipment /or materials; tutoring; classroom assistant services or alternative assessment practices; and curricular or instructional modification.

31. C: Cummins's quadrants go vertically from cognitively undemanding at the bottom to cognitively demanding at the top and horizontally from high-context (i.e., relevant to student experiences) at left to abstract at right. The bottom left quadrant A is cognitively undemanding and high context, and the top left quadrant B is high context and cognitively demanding. The top right quadrant C is cognitively demanding and abstract, and the bottom right quadrant D is abstract and cognitively undemanding. By starting with the abstract concept of alliteration without providing any personally relevant context for students, teacher 1 began in quadrant C. When he introduced the context of a poem to read, he moved to quadrant B. By starting with an existing poem and letting students find personal relevance in it, teacher 2 started in quadrant A. By having them discuss poetic techniques to discover alliteration on their own, she moved to quadrant B.

32. A: Repetition is one way of modifying language for English language learners (ELLs) without simplifying it. Paraphrasing is another (as long as alternative words and syntax are on levels equal to the originals). Using easier word choices (B) is simplification through modifying vocabulary. Speaking or reading aloud slower (C) is simplification through modifying speed. Exaggerating either the stressed syllables in words or the salient words in sentences (D) is simplification through modifying stress. Modifying intonation also would constitute simplification.

33. B: The inferential level of meaning infers the author's unstated meaning from events (or facts, images, symbols, or patterns) in reading selections; infers the main idea when not explicitly stated; identifies unstated reasons for acts (or statements or thoughts) according to explicit information; identifies implicit relationships; or predicts likely future actions, events, or results. In this example, the student infers from one spouse's dialogue to the other that the story ended happily for them. Choice (A) represents the literal level of meaning: The student essentially restates the content of the line of dialogue. Choice (C) is at the evaluative level of meaning by drawing a conclusion about the author's purpose or motivation for writing the ending. Choice (D) is also at the evaluative level by drawing a conclusion about the readers' values.

34. A: By calling on the first student to raise a hand, the teacher is not providing enough wait time for English language learner (ELL) students, who need longer times than native English-speaking students to process the question content, translate it into their L1s, formulate responses in their L1s, and then translate those responses into English before they are ready to raise their hands. All ELLs except those who have attained native-like English language proficiency (ELP) levels typically undergo this process. The question does not provide information to know whether the teacher frames his or her questions appropriately (B) or varies the types of questions he or she asks according to different student language needs (C); he or she may or not do these things. Hence, it is impossible to say whether the teacher needs to do these (D) or already does them.

35. B: The teacher gave implicit instruction in a metalinguistic learning strategy: By providing an example in Spanish of the sentence construction required English, he or she enabled the student to compare both languages and relate the understanding of Spanish conditional-subjunctive to an analogous English construction. If the student had been thinking about her own cognitive processes, how languages work in general, or how either Spanish or English works, she would have been using a more metacognitive (A) strategy. She learned a more metalinguistic strategy by

directly comparing two languages and equating a grammatical construction in both. This was not a vocabulary (C) strategy: The student was unfamiliar with both English and Spanish grammatical terms, having never received formal Spanish grammar instruction. It was not a translation (D) strategy: The Spanish and English terms are cognates; the student would easily recognize their similarity without needing to translate. The problem was that she did not know their grammatical meaning in either language. (Note: The teacher's instruction was more implicit than explicit: He or she did not explain conditional-subjunctive in either language but simply provided a Spanish-language example and let the student infer an equivalent English construction.)

36. A: This is an example of declarative memory, that is, the kind of memory that accumulates vocabulary words, phrases, and short sentences including idioms. Procedural memory (B) is the kind of memory that governs the process of applying morphological and grammatical rules to produce language. Episodic memory (C) is a subtype of declarative memory that involves remembering autobiographical events and experiences, including their times, places, other contextual elements, and the emotions associated with them. The other subtype of declarative memory is semantic memory, which describes the kind of declarative memory accessed in this example—vocabulary meanings, facts, knowledge, concepts, and so on. Because (A) is the only correct choice given, (D) is incorrect.

37. D: Providing realia from home countries of English language learner (ELL) students will stimulate students to explain, ask about, and explore characteristics and functions of these objects, generating relevant classroom conversations, which will further student English language development. Realia from other countries will not inform understanding of challenges to immigrant groups in the United States (A) as learning about topics like the naturalization process and discrimination would. Exposure to realia from their own and other students' home countries will not impede U.S. acculturation (B): The objects are in the classroom; students are still exposed to mainstream cultural objects throughout everyday life. Teaching object names in other languages will not interfere with English language development (ELD) in vocabulary (C): The children are conversing about objects in English and are otherwise required to use English inside and outside school. Also, many foreign-language words are sources of English vocabulary words; knowing some of these names can inform and enrich vocabulary knowledge in both other languages and English.

38. C: There is no need for the teacher to abandon his tradition (A) of telling a story for the students' enjoyment. Incorporating a holiday that only some English language learner (ELL) students observe (B) would exclude the other ELL students in the class. The teacher can modify the Thanksgiving celebration to a more universal family occasion, for example, a birthday, the birth of a new baby, and so on. Or he could make it a New Year celebration: Though different cultures may celebrate this on different dates (e.g., the Chinese New Year or Israeli or Jewish New Year), they generally do celebrate it. Continuing the tradition unchanged will enable ELL students to learn about U.S. culture (D), but it will not include the ELL students, which is what the question asks.

39. D: These two groups have differing academic needs. One has been exposed to academic language in their L1s; formal academic paradigms such as verb conjugations, mathematical formulae, scientific inquiry methods, assignments involving reading texts and writing compositions, and so in; the other has not. No information is given to indicate their specific cultural (A), linguistic (B),* or cognitive (C) needs differ in these ways. *One exception is that, linguistically, the students lacking previous formal education were not exposed to academic language in their L1s; however, learning academic English is a subcategory of learning all procedures associated with formal education, so academic needs is still the better choice.

40. C: Rosetta Stone, a popular language-learning system, has a Web site with interactive software including live lessons online, community-building activities, games, and son designed to teach learners how to speak foreign languages including English with native-like proficiency. The English as a second language (ESL) Jobs Forum (A) is a Web site for teachers of ESL to obtain information about training, teacher certification, job openings, and teaching. The Reading Plus system (B) is a web-based program designed to help students in Grade 3 and higher to improve not English speaking but reading proficiency including vocabulary, comprehension, silent reading, fluency, and standardized test scores. Easy Writer, from Software for Students (D), is a software application that uses authentic writing tasks to help English language learners (ELLs) develop their English writing, not speaking, proficiency.

41. A: To develop English language leaner (ELL) students' academic English in content-based English language development (ELD) instruction, the teacher needs to expose them to the maximum comprehensible English print materials possible. Selecting a grade-level text will assure they are learning content appropriate to fifth grade; adapting the syntax and vocabulary of the textbook to student English language proficiency (ELP) levels will make it comprehensible to them while also furthering their development of academic English. Avoiding print (B) will not give enough written English exposure. Substituting an outline for text (C) also limits print exposure. Selecting a lower grade-level text (D) will not provide appropriate grade-level content.

42. D: The interactive reading model emphasizes both interpretation skills, like making inferences and predictions, and word-level skills, like decoding (A). It regards reading as both proceeding from the parts to the whole (B) and from the whole to the parts (C). The interactive reading approach treats reading as a cognitive process that synthesizes information from both sensory and intellectual elements of reading.

43. B: Research shows that teaching early literacy strategies to English language learner (ELL) students who are refugees with little, interrupted, or no formal education is very effective, enabling them to progress by an average of eight reading levels within a single semester. This technique is not developmentally inappropriate (A) because these students lacked the preliteracy as well as literacy skills needed, even in their native languages (D). This instructional approach not only improved overall student achievement in reading but in receptive and expressive vocabulary as well (C).

44. D: According to California's explanation of its English language proficiency level descriptors (PLDs), English language learner (ELL) students at all levels of English language proficiency (ELP) can participate fully in grade-level work in any subject content area as long as they have appropriate amounts of scaffolding (support) for developing both English language skills and content area knowledge. ELL students at the first, emerging level are beginning to use academic English language (A). ELL students the second, expanding level are increasing and applying their language skills in more advanced, varied, age-appropriate, grade-level ways; however, they are typically not able to comprehend and produce highly technical texts (B) in English until they have reached the third, bridging level (C). This does not mean this level is the only one where students can participate fully; they can at all levels (D), provided they have applicable scaffolding.

45. C: The reading comprehension process this student has demonstrated most is identifying cause and effect in a text. The student accurately commented that the assassination triggered a series of occurrences leading up to World War I. This is more strongly associated with cause and effect than with making inferences (A) about things not stated in the text. Even if the text did not state the causal relationship explicitly; it arranged the events in chronological order and selected them to

show this relationship. This was less related to identifying facts and opinions (B) because the description refers only to events, which presumably were facts, and does not mention any author opinions. The student did not relate any of the events in the text to his or her own experiences (D) in the description.

46. C: This is an example of the revision aspect of the writing process. The student adds needed connective language and deletes verbiage that contributes no additional meaning. Organization (A) would involve things like starting with a thesis statement, beginning paragraphs with topic sentences, paragraphing appropriately to topic changes, and so on. Evaluation (B) would involve the student's coming up with a judgment about the value and effectiveness of his or her own composition. Focus (D) would involve clearly identifying the main point of the composition in advance, plus any supporting or related points, and then avoiding going off the subject by keeping the writing directed at the main point.

47. B: There are no grammatical errors in this sentence. There is a spelling (A) error where the word *first* is misspelled "frist." There are punctuation (C) errors where the comma is omitted following *Washington*, and the periods are omitted from *D.C.*, and there is a capitalization (D) error where *D.C.* is written in lowercase instead of capital letters.

48. D: When teachers plan Specially Designed Academic Instruction in English (SDAIE) lessons, they must include learning objectives for literacy (reading and writing) at grade level in the English language (A); for understanding and using academic English language (B)—both Tier II, general cross-curricular academic English and Tier III, subject-specific terminology; and also for knowing, understanding, analyzing, synthesizing, and evaluating content in the various required academic subjects at grade level (C).

49. B: The student made a connection between his previous knowledge from life experiences and the text he encountered in school because they shared common subject matter. The student can take advantage of this in accessing the student's previous knowledge. The teacher did not need to scaffold student–text interactions (A) because the student did not need it in this case. The example illustrates an independent student–text interaction, not a scaffolded teacher–student interaction (C). The teacher did not use strategies to create background knowledge (D), which already existed in this example.

50. D: Younger children are fascinated with real objects (A) and relate more to things they can see, touch, and physically manipulate (B) because their cognitive development is more concrete. Focus questions (C), though also useful when at a developmentally appropriate cognitive level, are still more abstract by nature than concrete objects.

51. D: It is not true that letting students speak in their L1s will interfere with their English language learning (A).Especially when English language learners (ELLs) have not yet attained good English proficiency, letting them communicate in their L1s will promote active use of language (C) and serve as a bridge to communicating in English. Cooperative learning tasks (B) will require students to communicate with one another to complete the work, which will also promote active language use.

52. C: Having the projects be original incorporates creativity; having them solve some problem incorporates critical thinking; having students plan and execute the projects as a joint effort incorporates collaboration and communication. Choice (A) incorporates critical thinking but not the other three Cs. Choice (B) incorporates critical thinking and collaboration and communication in

the planning stage but not in the execution stage but does not necessarily incorporate creativity. Choice (D) incorporates creativity and critical thinking and incorporates collaboration and communication in the execution stage but not in the planning stage. Thus, only (C) incorporates all four Cs throughout the entire activity.

53. A: To access students' prior knowledge, the most effective scaffolding strategy of the choices offered is to relate the new concepts and vocabulary words in English to ideas that are culturally familiar to English language learner (ELL) students and to equivalent or similar words in their native languages. Comparing the concepts to similar concepts that are also new in English and offering multiple word synonyms that are also English (B) do not access prior student knowledge: These only relate new material to other new material. Visual aids (C) are helpful for illustrating new concepts and words but may or may not access prior student knowledge depending on whether the visuals are familiar to them. Similarly, hands-on activities wherein students apply the new concepts and words (D) may or may not access their prior knowledge depending whether anything in the activities is familiar to them.

54. C: Of the choices offered, the best way to address English language learner (ELL) student needs when state-issued textbooks are provided for all students is to augment them with L1 translations. Giving ELLs subject-content texts issued for lower grade levels (A) is inappropriate: Though the language in these texts may be at a level more accessible to ELLs, they will not receive grade-level subject content. Condensing or summarizing texts (B) is a less acceptable way to modify textbooks as reducing English language reading at the expense of full text means ELLs will not get the same textbook content and features as other students. Replacing textbooks with visuals and objects (D) to avoid English language reading deprives ELLs of the practice they need to develop their English language reading skills for accessing subject content in English.

55. D: The question in (A) requires only factual knowledge, that is, remembering (or looking up) and reciting the six names of noble gases. Question (B) requires this same factual knowledge plus being able to categorize gases and differentiate noble gases from other kinds. Question (C) is similar to question (B) but is also outdated and inaccurate for using the term *inert*: Noble gases historically were considered inert but today are deemed relatively inert, that is, extremely stable and nonreactive, but it is not completely impossible for them to form compounds as previously thought. Question (D) requires the most critical thinking because students must apply knowledge of the stability of noble gases to answer "easy" or "hard" and then must additionally explain why, that is, because their octets or valence shells are filled with the maximum numbers of electrons, making them very stable and thus resistant to compounding. This question requires analysis, application, and interpretation as well as factual knowledge.

56. A: To frontload vocabulary, that it, pre-teach English language learners (ELLs) the vocabulary words used in a text that they will need to know in order to understand it before they read it, the first thing teachers need to do is to scan the text to identify the vocabulary words most likely to cause problems for these students. Research has revealed that, to comprehend text, students need a working knowledge of 95%—that is, most—of its vocabulary, not just 75% (B), so front-loading can be crucial for ELLs. An enormous help for identifying problem words in advance is to obtain student Lexile reading levels (C), which will give teachers an indication of which vocabulary they are likely to know and not know. Lexile Analyzer also will help teachers select specific texts (D) by scanning texts and returning their readability levels.

57. B: Research studies have found that giving English language learner (ELL) students explicit instruction in text genres in English helps them to improve their English writing skills. Hence, (A) is

incorrect. Studies also show that working with genres does help students to focus on text (C). Changing the genre of a given text to another genre involves producing a whole text, which is found to benefit both ELL and native English-speaking students (D).

58. B: The teacher should group English language learner (ELL) and native English-speaking students heterogeneously to give ELL students authentic opportunities to use English to communicate regarding academic content with both native and non-native English speakers. They should not be grouped homogeneously (A) as this will restrict their academic English communication to being only with other non-native English speakers. In some cases it may be reassuring and supportive to place at least two ELLs per heterogeneous group (C), but this is not always necessary and, in some classes, can be impossible depending on numbers of students. As heterogeneous grouping will give ELLs opportunities to communicate with both native and non-native English speakers and homogeneous grouping will not, it is incorrect that the grouping will make no difference (D).

59. A: Teachers should provide English language learner (ELL) students with feedback that is positive as well as corrective rather than only corrective feedback (B). Teachers' feedback also should be comprehensible, not in vocabulary above their level (C) and not unrelated to anything beyond the specific subject (D) but rather relevant to their lives to be meaningful to ELL students.

60. A: Long-term ELs, born in the United States to immigrant parents speaking only their native languages, have attended U.S. schools all their lives but with instruction so inadequate that their English skills—spoken, academic, or both—prevent school success. Under-schooled ELs, despite being in higher school grades, have had inadequate or interrupted instruction or have missed earlier grades in their home countries or the United States. Generation 1.5 ELs were born in another country, came to the United States around 12 years old, and began American education in middle or high school. By the time they are high school seniors, they have been educated in the United States for 6 to 10 years. Thus long-term ELs and Generation 1.5 ELs are likely to have spent more total time being educated in the United States. While some under-schooled ELs may have had equally long U.S. educations that were extremely inadequate, many others in this population have missed a lot of school, so this group overall is less likely to have as much total U.S. education time, and (D) is less likely.

CTEL 3

1. A: Research studies find many English language learner (ELL) students perform below their abilities academically. Investigators believe cultural disparities between school and home contribute to these achievement gaps. They recommend teachers address diverse learning approaches through culturally responsive instruction as a solution rather than concentrating on language at the expense of culture (B), attempting to change ELL students culturally through curricula (C), or homogeneously grouping ELL students according to their cultural backgrounds (D).

2. C: Gender roles, beliefs, values, mores, customs, worldviews, expectations, rituals and rites, nonverbal communication patterns, and work and leisure patterns are examples of internal elements of cultures. Family structures (B) also are examples of internal cultural elements, as are social roles (C) and status. Languages (A) are external, not internal elements of cultures, as are religious structures, governments, and technology; arts and literature; and food, shelter, and clothing.

3. B: Before the 1954 U.S. Supreme Court decision in *Brown v. Board of Education*, schools were racially segregated as either all white or all black; hence, classes within schools were not segregated (A). The basis of this landmark lawsuit was that black students were prohibited from attending white schools. Black schools were deemed "separate but equal." In *Brown v. Board of Education,* the Supreme Court ruled that segregated education was inherently unequal, overturning the antiquated "separate but equal" provision of *Plessy v. Ferguson* (1896). However, today there are actually some schools with 100% black student bodies and completely unequal educational standards (C). In the early 1950s, white schools did not exclude white immigrant students (D) the same way they excluded black American students.

4. A: Some hand gestures and body postures commonly accepted in America are viewed as insulting or prohibited in other cultures. Others are used in both cultures but convey different meanings. Nonverbal communication is an example of an internal element of culture. External elements of culture (B) include governments, religious structures, languages, and technologies and food, clothing, and shelter. Therefore, (C) and (D) are incorrect.

5. A: Social identity theory bases intergroup bias on a need for positive self-esteem, which in-group members derive from positive social identities. Social dominance theory (B) bases intergroup bias on social dominance orientation (SDO): Individuals with high SDO promote in-group domination of out-groups and intergroup hierarchies. Terror management theory (C) bases intergroup bias on a need for self-preservation: Individuals evaluate in-group members positively for holding similar cultural worldviews and out-group members negatively for threatening these. Optimal distinctiveness theory (D) bases intergroup bias on a need to assimilate and an equal, opposing need to differentiate: Individuals identify with groups offering the best balance of the two.

6. A: Assimilation refers to adjusting to a new culture by adopting its characteristics in favor of one's native cultural characteristics, being more or less absorbed into the new culture. Biculturalism (B) involves retaining elements of one's native culture while also adopting elements of the new culture, such that one identifies with two distinct cultures. Acculturation (C) is the process of adjusting and becoming acclimated to a new culture without necessarily assimilating into it or discarding one's native cultural elements. Accommodation (D) is a process of adding elements of a new culture into one's repertoire, adjusting native elements to allow elements of both cultures to coexist compatibly. Native cultural elements may be modified in admitting new cultural elements rather than being replaced by them as in assimilation.

7. C: In the honeymoon (A) or euphoric stage, English language learner (ELL) students are excited to learn about their new environment. In the culture shock stage (B), they become overwhelmed as they begin to realize all the cultural differences and have difficulty coping with surroundings and linguistic and social signals they cannot comprehend. In the integration stage (C), ELL students begin integrating new cultural elements. Some replace old values with new ones; others find ways to maintain both in peaceful coexistence. This is the stage wherein many immigrant parents first become alarmed about their children losing their original values and traditions. In the acceptance (D) stage, ELLs accept and may combine both cultures and can interact comfortably in mainstream culture. In this stage, many immigrant parents try to prevent their children from adopting mainstream culture for fear they will reject or forget their native cultures, which often happens.

8. D: Social distance, not psychological distance (B), refers to a student's degree of contact with a new language community. Psychological distance, not social distance (A), refers to a student's degree of comfort with learning a new language. Psychological distance is influenced by factors

including student motivation, culture shock, language shock, and individual ego permeability. Social distance is influenced by factors including student attitude, integration patterns, and cultural congruence (C) and social dominance, enclosure, cohesiveness, size, and the student's expected length of residence (D).

9. B: This exercise is designed to help students focus on exclusion: how we behave as part of a group, how it feels to reject outsiders, how it feels to be excluded, and when including some people and excluding others becomes a problem. This is not an activity focusing on diversity (A), that is, the differences among people; on prejudice (C), that is, biased opinions about groups or individuals based not on facts but on judgments; or on discrimination (D), that is, behaviors treating others unequally based on race, ethnicity, gender, class, sexual orientation, religion, and so on.

10. C: This student was raised in a collectivist culture typical of many Asian, Latin American, and other countries. American culture is individualistic, valuing competition and individual expression; collectivist cultures value cooperation above competition, often disapprove of individual expression, and advocate deferring one's own needs for the sake of group harmony and furthering the common good. Whereas the individual is paramount in the United States, in collectivist cultures, the group takes precedence. Rather than being intimidated, wanting to please her peers (A), trying to make new friends (B), or feeling inferior and afraid to compete (D) as motives, the most likely cultural reason for this student's behavior is to conform to the values of her native culture.

11. B: In 1965, the Immigration Act did away with the United States' former quota system, which had prevented many members of Asian, African, and other countries not in Europe from coming to America in larger numbers. The new law favored keeping families together by allowing immigration on a first-come, first-served basis. Therefore, after 1965, whole families were more likely to come to the United States than individuals. This law did not affect emigration from urban versus rural areas (A). Because Asian, African, Semitic, Hittite, and other languages were spoken by non-European immigrants, more people did not arrive speaking languages more similar to English (C), that is, Indo-European languages, after 1965 than before but vice versa. More immigrants did not arrive on the East Coast after 1965 (D): For example, many Chinese and other Asian immigrants settled in San Francisco and other places on the West Coast.

12. D: While immigrants in California have lower incomes than U.S.-born citizens—20.9% lower in 2011—and 18.9% are poor, while 15.7% of U.S.-born citizens are, immigrants have higher employment rates than U.S.-born citizens. As of 2011 figures, 62% of U.S.-born citizens versus 66% of immigrant citizens were in the civilian labor force. Fifty-nine percent of immigrants versus 54% of U.S.-born were likely to be employed. In the 2000s, fewer immigrants came to America than previously, not more (A), contributing to California's overall slower population growth. Roughly 81% of immigrants in California are age 18 to 64 years, not children (B); 57% of U.S.-born residents are adults. Hence, 34% of California's working-age citizens are immigrants. While 37% of immigrants versus 9% of U.S.-born in California had not completed high school in 2011, one-quarter of immigrants versus one-third of U.S.-born had college degrees; 72% of high school dropouts and 31% of college-educated California residents were immigrants. On the other hand, 47% of immigrants from 2007 to 2011 had bachelor's or higher degrees, and 60% of Asian immigrants did. Therefore, immigrants to California can have less or more education (C).

13. C: When people come to the United States from other countries to obtain better or more education (A), it is more often voluntary. When they migrate to find better-paying jobs or more sources of employment (B), some moves may be considered involuntary in the sense that they would rather stay in their home countries but cannot earn enough to support their families. But, the

pursuit of better work opportunities is still largely a voluntary reason for coming to America. When people move to America from other countries to be nearer to their family members (D) living here, these are generally voluntary moves. When people come to America fleeing terrorist regimes, to escape political persecution or imprisonment, to live in the greater political freedom of a democratic nation, or for other political (C) reasons, these are most often involuntary moves.

14. D: Research finds that losing their L1s does not benefit English language learner (ELL) students in acquiring the L2 (A). To the contrary, studies show that maintaining the L1 is important to aid ELL students for developing their vocabularies in the L2 (B), for the cognitive benefits they derive from bilingualism, and for the pride and self-confidence (C) they derive from retaining their original languages as the acquire a new one.

15. C: When assessing typically developing English language learner (ELL) students in their first languages, a consideration is that, as ELLs (unless very newly arrived), they have recently had less exposure to their L1s and more to English. Consequently, their L1 skills may be at an earlier level of development or have deteriorated with time. This puts them at risk of being overidentified as having developmental disorders or delays affecting language development. Additional considerations for L1 assessment is that standardized instruments are not as available here in L1s as they are in English (A); qualified practitioners to assess in L1s rather than English are also less available (B). ELLs are not as likely to be under-identified with language disorders or delays (D) as overidentified (C) when assessed in their L1s.

16. A: Experts advise that, for the purposes of assessing an English language learner (ELL) child's language abilities, full-time or three or more days weekly of exposure to English through school, day care, or babysitters constitutes significant, consistent exposure to the English language. However, incidental exposure to the English language from the television (B) or infrequent exposure to English language in the community (C) are considered casual, infrequent, and not qualifying as significant or consistent; exposure to English language spoken in the home (D) at the time of assessment does not qualify either.

17. B: Different cultures dictate different comfortable distances in social interactions. According to Lewis's Model of Cultural Types, Linear-Active cultures are cool, decisive, factual planners. These include England (A), the United States, Norway (B), Sweden, Germany, Estonia (C), and others. They tend to stand farther apart than Multi-Active cultures, which are emotional, impulsive, warm, and talkative. These include Italy (A), Greece, Spain, Brazil (B), Mexico, Russia, Croatia (D), and others. They stand closer when talking or interacting. Reactive cultures are polite, accommodating, compromising, and good listeners. These include China, Japan, Korea, Vietnam (D), Thailand, the Philippines, and so on. India is halfway between Multi-Active and Reactive, Canada halfway between Linear-Active and Reactive, and Belgium and Israel halfway between Linear-Active and Multi-Active. Hence, a Norwegian would be most uncomfortable if a Brazilian were standing too close during an interaction. The other choices are all the reverse of this relationship.

18. A: Americans have an individualistic culture, prizing autonomy most; Asians have a collectivist culture, prizing group harmony most. Americans speak more directly, candidly, and confrontationally, which they consider straightforward and honest. They use active voice. Asians would find this style shocking and embarrassing as well as impulsive, insensitive, rude, personally insulting, and even heartless. Asians would speak more indirectly and euphemistically, using more nonverbal communication and passive voice to avoid confronting and embarrassing others. Americans would find this style dishonest and irresponsible, that is, not taking responsibility for

one's words and actions, as well as evasive and unclear. Such cultural differences can cause misunderstandings, making intercultural communication challenging.

19. C: An appropriate intercultural communication strategy is to find out which terms are acceptable and unacceptable to certain cultural groups and then to use those terms to describe them that they find acceptable. If others use unacceptable terms to describe them, members of all cultural groups should say so and say what they want to be called. Rather than substituting Americanized names, which does not make newcomers feel welcome (A), it is important to learn the correct spelling, pronunciation, and sequence of the names that others want to be called and any applicable titles showing respect. Another strategy is to avoid applying generalizations about cultural groups to individuals from those groups (B). Rather than maintaining your usual interpersonal space (D), it is better to observe the space people from other cultures use when approaching you and adjust yours accordingly. Standing too close to or far from people from other cultures can cause them great discomfort.

20. B: Experts in cultural conflict prevention and resolution say that, rather than following the Golden Rule (A), that is, treating others the way we would like to be treated, it is better to follow the Platinum Rule, that is, treating others the way they would like to be treated. They find this analogous to not having sympathy, but rather empathy, or not walking in somebody else's shoes, but rather imagining how somebody else feels walking in his or her own shoes. This avoids conflict when the ways of different groups vary. Experts also advise that rather than a "when in Rome, do as the Romans do" approach, that is, conforming unquestioningly (C) to show respect, it is better to ask questions in an inquiry approach to learn about other cultures, instead of assuming we know things we do not, and to encourage growth and creativity rather than conformity, which excludes newcomers. They also remind us diversity is not only among different cultures (D) but within cultures; for example, they characterize the two biggest cultural groups as women and men. They find it more productive to assume all communications are cross-cultural in nature.

21. D: Because the new student is an English language learner (ELL), the teacher needs to assess the student's level of English language proficiency (ELP) before assigning interpretation of English literature (A). An academic contest (B) is a competitive activity that would not be congruent culturally for a student from a strongly collectivist culture that values cooperation above competition. Independent study (C) is more suited to the American individualist culture than to the group emphasis of a collectivist culture. A collaborative learning project (D) emphasizes group interdependence, which would be most culturally congruent for this student.

22. B: The teacher initially attributed the student's attitude to either linguistic or personal issues and overlooked the possibility of cultural causes because of her own cultural values, beliefs, and assumptions. This is why it is important for educators to examine their own cultural attitudes and what impacts they have on teaching culturally diverse students. Ignorance about the student's home culture (A) was a secondary reason; however, even not knowing about it, the teacher would more likely consider culture as a reason initially or investigate cultural reasons first were it not for her own cultural assumptions. The question does not include any information about the teacher's own childhood history (C). Knowing the student as a person (D) might or might not show the teacher the student was otherwise self-confident or comfortable with English-language speaking, but only by examining her own cultural assumptions could she consider culture as informing the student's attitude.

23. C: If the teacher wants to know specifically how an individual student's family observes cultural traditions related to social occasions and interactions, home visits with the family (including the

student) would allow the teacher both to observe their practices and to interview, ask questions, and converse with the family members about their customs. Informal conversation with the student could elicit the desired information, but conversing with the student's classmates (A) would not yield the same specific information and observations as visiting with the actual student and family and neither would interviewing other members of the culture's community (B). Reading books on the culture (D) would not inform the teacher of one family's specific practices as well as the family itself could.

24. C: To make the learning environment culturally responsive, schools can best inform their instructional practices by observing cultural differences in how diverse students approach learning and adjust teaching to be compatible with student approaches. English language development (ELD) instruction according to English language proficiency (ELP) level addresses students' EL skills and needs, but grouping them by background for content instruction (A) does not let them interact with native English-speaking students while learning and neither does homogeneous grouping (B). Alternating heterogeneous with homogeneous grouping does for half of the day (D) but does not accommodate instruction to students' culturally diverse learning styles.

25. B: Teachers can best support cultural diversity and student achievement equally by communicating equally high expectations of all students, which does not preclude providing appropriate cultural and linguistic accommodations to facilitate English language learner (ELL) student success. This is more effective than lowering expectations for ELLs in language (A), overall (D), or lowering expectations for all students to accommodate ELLs (C).

26. D: By showing interest in English language learner (ELL) students' L1s, allowing them to use their L1, and affirming it, the teacher most demonstrates respect for their cultural and linguistic diversity. Constantly correcting L1 use by telling them to use English (A) denies their linguistic diversity. Ignoring student L1 communications and selectively responding only to L2 use (B) does the same. Instructing ELLs to replace their cultural traditions with American practices (C) disrespects their cultural diversity.

27. C: Assigning cooperative group learning activities allows students of different backgrounds the highest levels of interaction for the most culturally inclusive learning environment. Assigning students to homogeneous groups with similar backgrounds (A) reduces interaction with students from other backgrounds. Assigning independent activities to prevent cultural conflicts (B) eliminates learning interactions with students from diverse backgrounds. Assigning students to the same pairs to expose each student to one partner's different background (D) limits each student to learning interactions with only one other student from a different background, instead of with many other students from different backgrounds.

28. A: Prejudice involves forming opinions of groups or individuals without any knowledge about them; discrimination involves treating certain groups or individuals differently than others in an unfair way. Prejudice more often involves thoughts; discrimination more often involves actions, not vice versa (B). Judging ahead of time is a literal meaning of the roots of the word *prejudice*; discrimination involving fine distinctions is a valid but separate meaning of the word *discrimination* or *discriminating* (C), as in matters of aesthetic tastes or sensibilities not applying to cultural conflict or treatment of other people. Prejudice and discrimination are related but are not exactly the same (D).

29. B: Experts advise that, to involve the parents of English language learner (ELL) students in the school, educators can arrange back-to-school events. When many parents in a community speak the

same non-English language, for example, Spanish in many communities, they advise hosting Spanish-language back-to-school evenings for these parents, including an interpreter, rather than holding them only in English (A). Similarly, school orientation tours for parents should include bilingual facilitators (B) to help communicate school information and answer parent questions. Many recent immigrant parents do not yet know of adult learning opportunities in which they may be interested, including English and native-language literacy classes; teachers can inform them of these without being perceived as condescending (C). Some ELL parents are able, willing, and interested to volunteer at the school (D). Teachers can recruit such parents according to their skills and interests as a way to involve them in the school.

30. D: By varying assignments among individual and collaborative work, a teacher can provide students with more flexibility in how they are assessed. Rather than assigning every student a project topic (A), the teacher can give them multiple topics from which they may choose for more flexibility. To accommodate different backgrounds, experiences, learning styles, and abilities, teachers can present information both orally and visually rather than only one or the other way (B). Rather than weighting all assignments toward final grades in advance (C), teachers can let students decide what percentage of their final grade they want each assignment to contribute at the beginning of the term or school year.

31. B: The most useful thing to know about English language learner (ELL) students' parents for making them feel welcome to become engaged with their children's educations is in which language they feel most comfortable communicating. By knowing this, educators can arrange for bilingual teachers or interpreters to be available so that parents are able to communicate most effectively and naturally during school visits and events. This knowledge has more practical application for interacting with parents than knowing their educational backgrounds (A), length of U.S. residence (C), or work histories and occupations (D).

32. C: If the educator does not know the English language learner's (ELL)'s family's language, he or she will not be able to conduct structured interviews (A) with them in their language or have informational conversations with them (B) in their language. He or she will also not be able to listen to or read written histories (D) from the family in their language. The educator's best choice of strategy would be to make use of community resources (C) to find other people who know the family's language and are willing to serve as interpreters and translators between the family and educator.

33. D: Community members are valuable resources for educators to involve in their schools and classrooms. They can contribute to student learning by sharing their insights about different cultural traditions (A); linguistic traditions (B), backgrounds, and information; and also the expertise in various content area subjects (C) that they possess.

34. D: Many public schools have School Governance Councils composed of school personnel, community members, students, and parents; some council memberships are 50% parents. They are not limited to school personnel (A), school personnel and community members (B), or school personnel, community members, and parents (C) without including the students, who must have a voice in their own education.

35. B: Basic principles of conflict management include that conflict is a necessary, normal, natural process (A); that every conflict style can have benefits in particular circumstances (B), which means that (C) is incorrect; and that conflict itself can be either destructive if we manage it dysfunctionally or productive if we manage it functionally, meaning that (D) is incorrectly stated.

36. C: The contributions approach incorporates activities and texts celebrating events, heroes, and holidays from different cultures, for example, learning about Dr. Martin Luther King, Jr.'s contributions during the month of January when his birthday is observed. While this approach includes issues and texts of cultural diversity, these are not required in the curriculum. The additive approach (B) adds multicultural perspectives, themes, concepts, and content into the curriculum without altering the existing curriculum structure by including literature about or by people from diverse cultural backgrounds. The transformation approach (D) does alter the curriculum structure by designing lesson units on cultural issues, themes, and concepts, including diversity as an essential premise and requiring critical thinking by students. The social action approach (A) takes the transformation approach one step further by including student activities that make efforts toward accomplishing social change, for example, writing letters to editors or Congress; community outreach and service projects; and so on.

37. A: According to experts, seven parameters to use as guidelines for transforming school curriculum to be multicultural are countries, cultures, and lives of origin; histories of oppression (B); works and contributions; implementers (C) and designers; global inclusiveness as well as local responsiveness (D); autobiographical (C) foundations; and student agency, social action, and authorship.

38. C: According to experts, one guideline for multicultural instruction is for educators to share autobiographical information relevant to their class content. For example, if a teacher has visited some students' native country, sharing this information can make students feel more at ease with the teacher, which can improve their class performance. Educators should share such experience not only in general terms (A) but also in ways pertinent to the class. Experts say that educators should also establish contexts in their classes wherein students are comfortable sharing their own personal perspectives (B). For example, a heterosexual teacher of a women's studies class that includes lesbian, gay, bisexual, and transgender (LGBT) issues could derive advantages through knowledge that some students who are openly lesbian, gay, bisexual, or transgender want to share their academic and personal perspectives on the content of the class.

39. A: The cultures identified are all more collectivist in contrast to America's individualist culture. The teacher can expect these students to value conformity more than individuality; to value cooperation more than competition, not vice versa (B); to be accustomed to less student talk, not more (C), and more teacher talk during teacher–student interactions; and to less student participation, not more (D) in class and lesson formats. For example, many Latin American countries use centralized curricula with a single set of textbooks; require school uniforms; and apply the same rules for all schools in the country. Some Asian cultures use more teacher-centered instruction, with students interacting and participating less than in American schools. Students from group-oriented cultures may find American customs of active, often noisy student participation in classes disrespectful when they first encounter them.

40. B: Considering this student's experiences, the teacher could best apply such knowledge by grading the student's classwork while in school instead of penalizing him for tardiness (A), (C) and grading the paper based on its content rather than its being turned in late (C), (D). This is more culturally responsive because, not only did the student make extra effort to attend school and complete an assignment despite difficulties he could not control (which often happens to Native American students who live on reservations or in poverty), but moreover, a knowledge of Native American cultures would inform the teacher that their values place meeting their commitments far above punctuality or adhering to rules. Hence, while an Anglo-American with these difficulties

might simply skip school and bring an excuse the next day, the Native American would honor his commitments to attendance and assignments no matter how long it took him to get there and to complete the work.

Practice Test #2

Practice Questions

CTEL 1

1. Spanish-speaking students learning English are finding it difficult to hear and pronounce the English phonemes /b/ and /v/ differently. The teacher gives them minimal pairs, like *bat* and *vat*, *buoyed* and *void*, to help them discriminate. What is his exercise a best example of?
    a. Phonics
    b. Phonology
    c. Articulation
    d. Morphology

2. A teacher with a class of English language learner (ELL) students from Japan finds the students have trouble pronouncing English words featuring consonant clusters, for example, *strike*. They tell her that, in their language, this word is *sutoraiku*. From the Japanese version of the word, how can the cause of their difficulty be inferred?
    a. They are generalizing the difference in these two words to all English words.
    b. Their native language excludes one or more of the consonants in the cluster.
    c. Their native language never clusters but separates consonants with vowels.
    d. They are accustomed to consonant clusters only in certain positions in words.

3. English language learner (ELL) students at the intermediate level of English language development display writing errors such as the underlined part of the following: "She likes to ski, skate, and <u>snowboarding</u>." To help them correct this type of error, the teacher should work with them on which of these?
    a. Usage of gerunds
    b. Parallel structure
    c. Use of infinitives
    d. Indirect objects

4. A student learning English as a second language tends to speak and write English sentences without *the* or *a* before nouns, for example, "I have book" and "We are sitting at desk." What does the teacher need to give the student instruction about?
    a. Using articles
    b. Definite articles
    c. Indefinite articles
    d. Demonstrative adjectives

5. Which of the following is an example of how choices among language variations are influenced by various types of discourse?
a. A bilingual teacher asks English language learner (ELL) students' parents their language preference during conferences.
b. A student learns to speak in different words and constructions with adults than with friends.
c. An ELL student spells words correctly in writing but pronounces them incorrectly in speaking.
d. An individual relocated to a different American region keeps his or her original regional dialect.

6. A teacher has given a class of English language learner (ELL) students some sample essay texts to analyze. They analyze and discuss whether each essay organizes its ideas well and produces a sense of unity through using a thesis statement and topic sentences throughout. What is the teacher instructing the students in?
a. Cohesion
b. Coherence
c. Both of these
d. Neither of these

7. Of the following, which does a student need to attend to most to become pragmatically competent in his or her writing?
a. The purpose of the writing and the target reading audience
b. The structure of the writing and the way that it is organized
c. The relative level of complexity in the syntax of the writing
d. The degree of specificity in the writer's vocabulary choices

8. Among the following types of academic essays, which one is MOST likely to use comparison and contrast or cause and effect to explain a process to the reader?
a. Narration
b. Description
c. Exposition
d. Persuasion

9. Which of the following words have Latin roots?
a. Pentagon, peptic, pharmacy
b. Penalty, punish, penitentiary
c. Page, pediatric, pedagogical
d. Pandemic, phantom, phlegm

10. Which of these English words have Greek origins?
a. Pedal, pedestrian, or centipede
b. Pending, pendulum, appendage
c. Perfectly, persistence, permeate
d. Periscope, perimeter, peripheral

11. Of the following, which root is found in both Greek and Latin, spelled the same but with different word origins and meanings?
    a. Cirr-
    b. Cine-
    c. Circ-
    d. Circum-

12. Which pair of English words is descended from the same origin?
    a. Edible and obese
    b. Emetic and emulate
    c. Exclude and exempt
    d. Ecumenical and ecclesiastical

13. What is the MOST significant reason for learning Greek and Latin roots for English words?
    a. To pass English language arts tests
    b. To impress others with one's knowledge
    c. To be able to figure out new word meanings
    d. To enable English language learner (ELL) students to recognize cognates

14. People who misspell the word *versus* as "verses," which has a different meaning, MOST reveal an ignorance of underlying:
    a. spelling.
    b. etymology.
    c. morphology.
    d. B and C.

15. An English language learner (ELL) student is able to determine that the word *bear* means to carry rather than a big animal because it is used as a verb and has an object of *burden* in a sentence. This is an example of which vocabulary and semantics strategy?
    a. Apposition
    b. Context clues
    c. Word structure
    d. Prior L1 knowledge

16. Which of the following is accurate regarding the California State Board of Education Adopted Reading/Language Arts-English-Language Development (RLA/ELD) Programs?
    a. Not all of them are aligned with standards.
    b. All of these programs are Basic programs.
    c. All are Intensive Intervention programs.
    d. Not all of them target English learners.

17. An English language learner (ELL) student says, "I will come for your house." What is this error regarding?
    a. Adjectives
    b. Prepositions
    c. Conjunctions
    d. Indirect objects

18. A class of advanced-level, high school English language learner (ELL) students is analyzing a piece of text their teacher has given them that uses a highly convoluted writing style filled with long, compound-complex sentences containing multiple clauses, modifiers nested within modifiers, and so on. While the text described involves all four of the following, which one does the description refer to MOST specifically?
    a. Writing style
    b. Level of difficulty
    c. Complexity of syntax
    d. Featured language structures

19. In the scoring rubric for the Short Compositions item on the Grades 2 through 12 Writing test of the California English Language Development Tests (ELDTs), which of the following is one criterion included for assigning a score of 4—Fully Competent Communication?
    a. The response contains well-organized ideas and events, a few effective details, and transitional devices.
    b. The response has logical sequencing and is mostly recognizable and comprehensible as a paragraph.
    c. The response has correct subject and predicate word order in at least one complete or run-on sentence.
    d. At least one word (not *a, I,* or *the*) is spelled correctly, and the subject and predicate is recognizable.

20. Of the following, which have research studies found about how English language learners (ELLs) apply pragmatics knowledge socially?
    a. They more often interpret others' speech literally than infer meaning from the context.
    b. They tend to use politeness markers more in English than they typically would in their L1.
    c. They tend to be more sensitive to context in choosing pragmatic strategies in L2 than L1.
    d. They are more likely to exaggerate context factors of social power and distance in English.

21. A teacher evaluates the California English Language Development Tests (CELDTs) for addressing areas of phonology and morphology. On these tests, which question does the teacher identify as MOST addressing phonological production?
    a. Choose and give reasons
    b. Short compositions
    c. Speech functions
    d. Copying letters

22. A teacher gives English language learning (ELL) students three sentences: "She knew what to do." "She knew what not to do." "She knew not what to do." Student 1 thinks these all have the same meaning. Student 2 notices that the second and third sentences contain a negative that the first sentence does not but thinks the second and third sentences mean the same thing. Student 3 correctly says they all have different meanings. What is this exercise an example of?
    a. Applying syntactic clues to determine semantics
    b. Applying semantic clues to determine syntactics
    c. Applying syntax and semantics to determine grammar
    d. Applying syntax and semantics to determine vocabulary

23. In the California English Language Development Tests (CELDTs), which of the following test items MOST addresses the social functions of language?
    a. Word analysis
    b. 4-Picture narrative
    c. Reading comprehension
    d. Choose and give reasons

24. A teacher explains to advanced English language learner (ELL) students that some words with one spelling have different meanings and parts of speech depending on syllable stress, for example, *prog*ress and pro*gress, ob*ject and ob*ject, pro*duce and pro*duce,* and so on. What is the MOST significant aspect reflected by this phenomenon?
    a. The difference between English nouns and verbs
    b. A difference between written and spoken English
    c. A difference in the orthographies of English words
    d. A similarity between spellings and pronunciations

25. The teacher of an English language learner (ELL) class has assigned every student an oral presentation on an academic subject, and every student has completed this assignment. Now the teacher assigns them different oral presentations to prepare: This time, they are to treat personal subjects like pets, hobbies, family members, friends, and social activities; use informal styles and registers; and incorporate humor and play through jokes, funny anecdotes or puppets; theatrical elements like costumes and makeup; body movements, dialogue, role-play, and so in. In terms of pragmatics, what is the teacher's MOST likely purpose in making this assignment?
    a. To get the students to loosen up and stop acting so serious all the time
    b. To promote oral discourse suitable to different contexts and audiences
    c. To provide instruction in entertaining others to fit in and gain popularity
    d. To give students a break from the tedium of studying academic English

26. Among the following theorists, which one is MOST associated with the idea that people are born with internal capacities to learn and produce language?
    a. Skinner
    b. Chomsky
    c. Vygotsky
    d. Chapman

27. When a student learns to identify different parts of speech like nouns, verbs, adjectives, adverbs, and so on, which of the following cognitive processes does this MOST demonstrate?
    a. Memorization
    b. Categorization
    c. Generalization
    d. Metacognition

28. Which of these reflects a valid finding about first- and second-language acquisition?
    a. The sequence and stages of learning are the same with first and second languages.
    b. Receptive language precedes expressive language in L1s but is the opposite in L2s.
    c. Overgeneralization of vocabulary or grammatical rules is done only by children in L1.
    d. In both L1s and L2s, the only basis of acquisition learners have is universal grammar.

29. In the Acquisition-Learning hypothesis of Krashen's theory of second-language acquisition, which of these is correct?
    a. Acquisition is unconscious, and learning is conscious.
    b. Acquisition is conscious, and learning is unconscious.
    c. Acquisition and learning both mean the same thing.
    d. Acquisition is not as important as natural learning is.

30. Which of the following statements is accurate regarding Krashen's theory of second-language acquisition?
    a. The Monitor hypothesis involves both acquisition and learning.
    b. The Input hypothesis also entails both acquisition and learning.
    c. The Natural Order hypothesis should dictate L2 teaching order.
    d. The Affective Filter hypothesis says affect by itself enables L2.

31. According to Krashen's Monitor hypothesis, which is NOT a condition of the monitor's planning, correcting, and editing functions?
    a. The L2 learner must have enough time for use.
    b. The L2 learner focuses on correctness or form.
    c. The L2 learner makes major use of the monitor.
    d. The L2 learner has to know the language rules.

32. English language learner (ELL) student Sami notices a quizzical look on an American classmate's face after he has made a comment in English that his classmate does not recognize. Sami realizes he has just translated a common expression from his native language into English without thinking about it. He explains to his classmate that they often say this in his language and what it means. This is MOST an example of which strategy?
    a. Repetition
    b. Elaboration
    c. Self-monitoring
    d. Formulaic expressions

33. A multilingual teacher is instructing English language learner (ELL) students in English grammar. A Spanish-speaking student attempts an exercise, making a common grammatical error. The teacher then speaks to him in Spanish to instruct him in the specific grammatical point, which is analogous in both languages. What strategy does this illustrate?
    a. Code-switching using prior L1 learning to inform L2 learning
    b. Role-playing giving a student practice in real-life English use
    c. Requesting clarification to make something in English clearer
    d. Appealing for assistance about the English grammatical point

34. English language learner (ELL) students who develop their skills for _____ and _____ in English typically find it easier to _____ and _____ in English.
    a. Writing, listening; read, speak
    b. Speaking, writing; listen, read
    c. Listening, reading; speak, write
    d. Reading, writing; listen, speak

35. Which is accurate regarding comparative characteristics of Basic Interpersonal Communication Skills (BICS) versus Cognitive Academic Language Proficiency (CALP)?
    a. English language learner (ELL) students require CALP for social communication.
    b. ELL students typically acquire BICS faster than CALP.
    c. ELL students need BICS to use for academic reasons.
    d. ELL students with good BICS are proficient in English.

36. On the California English Language Development Tests (CELDTs), a score of 3 on the Grades 3 through 5 Writing test Short Compositions question indicates which of these descriptors?
    a. Emerging communication
    b. Developing communication
    c. Fully competent communication
    d. Competent communication

37. A student acquiring a second language has a very strong auditory orientation in learning. This enables him to discriminate phonological differences between L1 and L2, articulate L2 phonemes accurately, and quickly develop a native-sounding accent in the L2. It also helps him remember new vocabulary words, syllabic word stress, and grammatical structures by their sounds. Among factors affecting L2 development, which does this example illustrate?
    a. Cognitive styles
    b. Language transfer
    c. Previous knowledge
    d. Physiological factors

38. A class of first-grade, beginning English language learner (ELL) students cannot engage in English-language conversations with one another. Their teacher regularly provides them with enough support to enable them to conduct basic English conversations in pairs and then in small groups. As they develop more proficiency with conversational English, the teacher gradually decreases the amount of support. Little by little, the students improve until they are able to engage independently in basic English conversations. What pedagogical process does this describe?
    a. Assessing language proficiency
    b. Providing constructive feedback
    c. Building on student L1 knowledge
    d. Scaffolding language learning tasks

39. Which teacher practice MOST creates a supportive learning environment conducive to English language development for students learning English as a new language?
    a. The teacher consistently gives immediate, explicit feedback to identify and correct all student errors.
    b. The teacher ignores errors not interfering with meaning but consistently rephrases significant errors.
    c. The teacher gives the most feedback to students making the highest number and severity of errors.
    d. The teacher selectively corrects students only when interference from their L1s is not causing errors.

40. Of the following, which school practice is MOST conducive to English language development for students from other countries?
    a. Getting students' parents to learn and speak only English at home
    b. Total-immersion English instruction and American school activities
    c. Linguistically inclusive instruction and multicultural school activities
    d. Helping students adopt mainstream culture via enriched activities

41. Regarding bilingual language development, which of the following beliefs have research studies MOST supported?
    a. Bilingual language development does not hinder either language and can afford cognitive benefits.
    b. Bilingual language development is harmless when sequential but, when simultaneous, is confusing.
    c. Bilingual language development is harmless when simultaneous but, when sequential, is confusing.
    d. Bilingual language development, simultaneous or sequential, slows development in each language.

42. When English language learner (ELL) students use code-switching (i.e., while speaking English, switching to their L1 for a certain word or phrase), which function of code-switching is MOST likely when both languages do not each have a word with the same or culturally equivalent meaning?
    a. Reiteration
    b. Equivalence
    c. Floor holding
    d. Conflict control

43. Two English language learner (ELL) students are perplexed encountering the English idiom "beat around the bush." Their multilingual teacher explains that, in French, one student's L1, its meaning is like *tourner autour du pot,* that is "go around in circles" (literally "stir around the pot"); and in Norwegian, the other student's L1, it is like *å gå som kata rundt den varme grauten,* that is, literally "pace around hot porridge like a cat." Both students' faces light up with understanding. This is an example of which factor that affects L2 development?
    a. Negative language transfer
    b. Language proficiency level
    c. Prior student knowledge
    d. Cognitive and learning styles

44. Which of these is true regarding first- and second-language acquisition?
    a. Older L2 learners have the benefit of metacognition.
    b. Age only affects proficiency in L2 but not L1 learning.
    c. Universal grammar influences older L2 learners more.
    d. Older L2 learners are more sensitive to L2 phonology.

45. Which distinction between L1 and L2 learning is MOST valid?
    a. L2 learners are just as likely to achieve native-like proficiency in the L2 as L1 learners are.
    b. L1 learners, unlike L2 learners, always achieve native proficiency in their own languages.
    c. L1 learners with language-related learning disabilities may not achieve native proficiency.
    d. L2 learners typically have equal chances as L1 learners for authentic learning and practice.

46. In the Grades 2 through 12, performance descriptors of proficiency levels of the California English Language Development Tests (CELDTs), which level includes the description, "Errors still complicate communication"?

    a. Beginning
    b. Intermediate
    c. Early advanced
    d. Early intermediate

47. For English language learner (ELL) students to succeed in writing English, which is the BEST instructional approach?

    a. For them to begin writing in English before any other tasks
    b. For them to practice speaking English before writing English
    C. For them to listen to plenty of spoken English before writing
    d. For them to develop some proficiency in reading English first

48. Which of the following is MOST correct regarding an English language learner (ELL) student's needs in school?

    a. A student functioning well socially in English needs Basic Interpersonal Communication Skills (BICS) for a calculus course.
    b. A student who needs to learn how to have English conversations needs Cognitive Academic Language Proficiency (CALP).
    c. A student feeling isolated and friendless due to a language barrier needs BICS.
    d. A student needs CALP in a social studies seminar that requires 100% discussion.

49. For an English language learner (ELL) student whose family has recently immigrated to the United States and who appears inhibited about communicating in English, which teacher strategy is MOST likely to lower the student's affective filter?

    a. Validating the student's home culture and language
    b. Directing focus to mainstream culture and language
    c. Lowering the academic expectations of this student
    d. Delivering exclusively corrective language feedback

50. Javier's family recently came to America, fleeing from a terrorist regime in Honduras. Nakul's family came from a big city in India, where he attended school since age three. Which can BEST be inferred from this information?

    a. Javier is more likely to be electively bilingual; Nakul is more likely to be circumstantially bilingual.
    b. Javier is likely more English proficient because Spanish is more like English than Indian languages.
    c. Nakul is likely more English proficient because Indian schools have taught English for generations.
    d. Nakul and Javier are about equally likely to have similar motivation for and proficiency in English.

Constructed-Response

1. Describe a cognitive or linguistic factor that influences second-language acquisition (e.g., learning styles, prior knowledge, positive and negative language transfer, or previous school experience). Describe one instructional strategy for English language learner (ELL) students to address the factor you described.

Explain how this strategy furthers ELL language learning relative to the factor you described.

CTEL 2

1. In Wiggins and McTighe's Backward Design principles for lesson planning, which of the following is included in Stage 2?
    a. Which essential knowledge and skills the students will understand
    b. Which criteria will be used for judging student understandings
    c. Which content standards will be met by the teaching design
    d. Which experiences will help students achieve results

2. When differentiating English language arts (ELA) instruction and assessment for English language learner (ELL) students, what most relates to giving ELLs multiple opportunities to learn?
    a. Using a variety of methods for frequently monitoring whether students understand target concepts
    b. Setting up instructional sessions especially designed to prepare students for unfamiliar test situations
    c. Reinforcing communication modes students will need to understand and use for standardized exams
    d. Combining oral and written directions with real objects, manipulatives, and graphics to explain concepts

3. Which of these is the MOST appropriate use of a summative assessment?
    a. Determining at the end of a unit if students achieved state standards on which instruction is based
    b. Determining during instruction whether students are making sufficient progress to meet standards
    c. Determining how to modify ongoing instruction so it will more effectively address students' needs
    d. Determining how to design further differentiated, standards-based instruction for given students

4. Of the following statements, which is MOST true about California English language proficiency level descriptors (PLDs) standards?
    a. English language arts (ELA) standards were established after English language development (ELD) standards were developed.
    b. ELD standards are similar to ELA standards at every level of proficiency.
    c. ELD standards are similar to ELA standards only at the advanced level.
    d. ELA standards and ELD standards are completely different at all levels.

5. How does Wiggins and McTighe's Backward Design differ from other instructional planning processes?
   a. Teachers have to plan a range of assessments before planning learning experiences.
   b. Teachers have to plan learning experiences and a range of assessments concurrently.
   c. Teachers have to replace traditional assessments with authentic performance tasks.
   d. Teachers have to plan learning experiences first and assessments at the end of units.

6. An English language test gets very similar results across repeated administrations to native English-speaking students but widely varying results when administered repeatedly to English language learner (ELL) students. What is this assessment issue MOST related to?
   a. Validity
   b. Reliability
   c. Test bias
   d. All these

7. A class including both native English-speaking and English language learner (ELL) students is given an English language arts (ELA) test. All of the ELL students score significantly lower, that is, greater than two standard deviations below all of the native English-speaking students. Analyzing the item scores, teachers discover the ELL students performed at grade level in all English language development (ELD) areas—vocabulary words, grammar, fluency, and so on, but the test contained an excessive number of idiomatic expressions unfamiliar to them. Which statement best represents this assessment issue?
   a. This test was biased by too much content ELLs could not be expected to know.
   b. This test was unreliable because ELLs scored much lower than native students.
   c. This test was invalid because the ELLs scored greater than two standard deviations below the other students.
   d. This test was unbiased, reliable, and valid and revealed a weakness of the ELLs.

8. On the California English Language Development Tests (CELDTs), the ELD standard, "Listen attentively to stories and information and identify important details and concepts by using both verbal and nonverbal responses," is referenced for an item on one of the tests. Under which category is this item found?
   a. Following oral directions
   b. Oral vocabulary
   c. Teacher talk
   d. Rhyming

9. Which of the following is accurate regarding the California High School Exit Examination (CAHSEE)?
   a. The English language arts (ELA) part of the CAHSEE is aligned with California academic content standards through Grade 12.
   b. The ELA part of the CAHSEE has reading and writing tests both with multiple-choice and essay items.
   c. The ELA part of the CAHSEE tests vocabulary, reading, information and literary analysis, and writing.
   d. The ELA part of the CAHSEE's writing task requires a written response to passages of literature only.

10. Of the following, which reflects correctly the criteria used by the California State Board of Education for releasing past questions from the California Standards Test (CST) as samples to guide teachers' classroom assessments and students' preparations?

    a. Questions selected for release test content standards for that grade's English language arts (ELA) test.

    b. Questions selected for release demonstrate a reasonably uniform level regarding difficulty.

    c. Questions selected for release have to show a relatively consistent way to assess standards.

    d. Questions selected for release must include no more than 1% to be reused on future tests.

11. A teacher's classroom includes both native English-speaking and English language learning (ELL) students. The ELL students are at a variety of different English language proficiency (ELP) levels. To use the most appropriate classroom assessment to monitor the ELL students' progress, what will be the most immediate, easy, and effective strategy?

    a. Ask the school district to provide alternative benchmarks for the ELL students.

    b. Ask the school district to provide alternative textbooks with easier assessments.

    c. Differentiate the levels of discussion questions to check all students' understanding.

    d. Differentiate the levels of instruction to allow the ELL students better understanding.

12. When conducting informal assessments of English language learning (ELL) students at beginning English language development (ELD) levels, which of the following is a limitation of a method whereby students identify the correct picture among several to answer questions?

    a. Students do not have to speak but can still communicate correct responses.

    b. Students do not have opportunities to elaborate or explain their responses.

    c. Students do not have to detract from performance with inadequate speech.

    d. Students do not have to risk accidental wrong meanings via wrong word use.

13. A student is enrolled in an American school, having just arrived from another country days before. He never heard English in his isolated home village and was never exposed to it via TV, radio, the Internet, and so on. His native language differs radically from English. An educational specialist who speaks his language gives him a battery of tests in his L1 and reports his IQ and other scores are intellectually and adaptively in the top 1% of the population. In addition to English language learner (ELL) instruction, which referral is most indicated?

    a. Student study team (SST)

    b. Gifted and talented education (GATE)

    c. Special education

    d. Intervention programs

14. If a student is identified with both English language learner (ELL) status and visual impairment, which of the following classroom interventions or modifications will NOT address the student's needs best?

    a. Differentiating instruction for the language level

    b. Preferential seating at the front of the classroom

    c. Magnifiers, large-print text, and audio recordings

    d. More reading or written than heard or oral assignments

15. Which of the following is an example of scaffolding content-area assessment tasks for English language learner (ELL) students?

    a. Providing ELL students with a glossary of English chemistry terms to write their experiment report

    b. Providing ELL students with an English thesaurus while they write a descriptive essay for ELA class

    c. Providing ELL students with guiding questions and writing models for their narrative compositions

    d. Providing ELL students with pictures for reference in responding with vocabulary word definitions

16. English language learner (ELL) educational programs in California are required to provide which of these at every grade level?

    a. Specially Designed Academic Instruction in English (SDAIE) and content-based English language development (ELD)

    b. Development in the primary language and content-based ELD

    c. Support in the primary language and ELD

    d. Access to the core curriculum and ELD

17. Among equity issues related to educating English language learners (ELLs), which of the following are documented occurrences?

    a. ELLs are denied gifted education program placement because language barriers obscure their gifts.

    b. ELLs are wrongly placed in special education programs because language barriers are misconstrued.

    c. ELLs are systematically placed in classrooms with teachers less qualified than others in their school.

    d. ELLs are documented to have experienced all of these educational equity issues as well as others.

18. English language learner (ELL) students A and B are currently in the same grade. Both have equal, grade-level English language proficiency (ELP) in listening, speaking, and reading. Student A is two years below grade level in writing; Student B is one year below grade level in writing. Student B had several years more of formal education in her home country than Student A. Student B has tested at the same ELP level for writing on the California English Language Development Tests (CELDTs) for three years. Student A moved up one grade level in writing ELP on last year's CELDTs. Which choice represents the MOST appropriate writing program and rationale for these students?

    a. Student A and Student B should receive the same writing instruction to reach grade level this year.

    b. Student B should find it easier to move up another grade in writing as she did in the previous year.

    c. Student A needs more rigorous instruction to move her writing ELP up two years within this year.

    d. Student B can handle more rigorous instruction due to more formal school and longer ELP years.

19. Among the following English language learner (ELL) student descriptions, which one should be placed in content-based English language development (ELD) instruction rather than Specially Designed Academic Instruction in English (SDAIE)?
    a. A third-grader, far below basic education level, at an early-intermediate ELD level
    b. A seventh-grader, far below basic education level, at the intermediate ELD level
    c. A tenth-grader, below the basic education level, at an intermediate level of ELD
    d. All of these ELL students

20. A teacher has a new English language learner (ELL) student placed in a mainstream English classroom. The student's parents have just immigrated to America, speak little or no English, and have no formal education in their native language. The teacher, who is bilingual in the parents' native language, wants to inform them of their rights, for example, to request alternative programs, parental exception waivers, and so on. Which of the following would be the most appropriate and effective choice of medium for communicating these rights?
    a. Mailed English-language documents
    b. An English e-mail summary of rights
    c. A bilingual phone call or home visit
    d. Mail or e-mail in their native language

21. Several English language learner (ELL) students in the same class came to America months before being enrolled in school. They acquired experience with conversing in English during the interim but have less experience and facility with reading written English. Which supplemental material or activity and the teacher provide that will facilitate their using their proficiency with listening to English oral language to promote English literacy?
    a. Providing lists of vocabulary words used in their reading with L1 translations
    b. Providing audio recordings of books read aloud to accompany their reading
    c. Providing text in English with the L1 translation of it for side-by-side reading
    d. Providing paired reading assignment within the same group of ELL students

22. An English language learner (ELL) student had many friends in his home country and was more socially than academically inclined. While he understood and spoke no English upon recently arriving in America, he acquired good conversational English skills in a very short time and soon made many friends here. While academic English typically takes longer to develop, he also was less interested in acquiring it. Which personal factor affecting EL literacy development does this MOST illustrate?
    a. Motivation
    b. Vocabulary knowledge
    c. Background experiences
    d. English language proficiency (ELP) level

23. In Marzano's Six-Step Vocabulary Process to help build academic vocabulary, which step is involved when students draw a picture to illustrate definitions of words?
    a. Step 6, Games
    b. Step 5, Discussion
    c. Step 2, Linguistic definition
    d. Step 3, Nonlinguistic definition

24. Which of the following scaffolding strategies or approaches for developing English language learners' (ELLs') cross-curricular English language reading and writing proficiency are typically most visual and nonlinguistic in nature?

    a. Learning logs
    b. Shared reading
    c. Graphic organizers
    d. Interactive journals

25. Among the following scaffolding strategies to support student text interaction, which one is used only after reading?

    a. Role, audience, format, topic (RAFT)
    b. Question–answer relationships (QAR)
    c. The questions-only strategy for reading
    d. The reader's–writer's notebook strategy

26. In an interdisciplinary instructional unit for ninth graders based on California standards and organized around the theme that perspective influences human perception, communication, and understanding, one set of three learning objectives is taught by teachers of three different subjects. Which of the following learning objectives represents the English portion of the unit?

    a. Students will use sensory details, suitable modifiers, and precise wording.
    b. Students will know how antibodies are involved in responses to infection.
    c. Students will evaluate strategies to manage influences on substance use.
    d. Not enough information is provided in these examples to determine this.

27. According to the California Reading and Language Arts Framework, the difficulties or needs of these students "must be addressed quickly to prevent [them] from falling behind." Which group does this describe?

    a. Strategic Group
    b. Intensive Group
    c. Benchmark Group
    d. Special Needs Group

28. When a teacher develops lesson objectives, which of the following demonstrates one that addresses both English language development (ELD) standards and content standards for English language learner (ELL) students?

    a. The student will show understanding of the social studies concepts listed (this includes a list).
    b. The student will define the economics vocabulary terms included in the social studies course.
    c. The student will define economics vocabulary from the social studies course in written English.
    d. The student will explain social studies concepts and economics terms listed in written English.

29. A teacher has a number of English language learner (ELL) students within a mainstream English language classroom. These students are at intermediate (mainstreamed at parental request), early-advanced, and advanced levels of English language proficiency (ELP). Which of the following strategies could the teacher MOST easily use to support their learning?

    a. Technologies
    b. Peer tutoring
    c. Team teaching
    d. Paraprofessionals

30. Regarding how teachers can engage parents of English language learner (ELL) students when the parents lack English language skills and the teacher does not speak their language, which of these is true?

    a. The teacher's learning some common words and phrases in their language will do no good.

    b. The teacher should use the student to translate rather than look for a bilingual interpreter.

    c. The teacher's giving contacts of bilingual staff seems like passing the parents off to others.

    d. The teacher can inform parents of adult literacy learning opportunities in their community.

31. According to Cummins' quadrants model, in which quadrant would students encounter tasks that were easy to perform yet abstract in nature and unrelated to students' real lives?

    a. Quadrant A

    b. Quadrant B

    c. Quadrant C

    d. Quadrant D

32. For English language learner (ELL) students in kindergarten through Grade 1, which of the following strategies to scaffold tasks requiring academic language proficiency would be MOST developmentally appropriate?

    a. Realia

    b. Analogies

    c. Manipulatives

    d. Both (A) and (C)

33. High school students have just read a story in which the final sentence is, "They all lived happily ever after." One student comments, "After everything that happened in the story, this ending is unrealistic!" At which level of meaning is this comment?

    a. Literal

    b. Inferential

    c. Evaluative

    d. None of these

34. For English language learner (ELL) students who have developed grade-level English language vocabulary but are below grade level in their comprehension of spoken English syntax, how should a teacher vary the types of questions he or she asks the students aloud in class?

    a. Ask questions using simple sentences.

    b. Ask questions using simpler word choices.

    c. Ask questions using a smaller range of words.

    d. Ask questions using simpler structures and words.

35. A teacher using Specially Designed Academic Instruction in English (SDAIE) with high school English language learner (ELL) students not only teaches them subject content and English language skills but additionally gives them explicit instruction in categorizing words by their syntactic and semantic characteristics. How will this help the students develop their subject content and English language knowledge?

    a. It will enable them to distinguish the main and supporting ideas better.

    b. It will enable them to understand and remember English words better.

    c. It will enable them to preplan and organize their compositions better.

    d. It will enable them to feel less anxious and perform English tasks better.

36. An English language learner (ELL) student has just learned the English word *focus*. Without further instruction, she is able to say, "This week we focus on the Civil War in American history. Last month we focused on the Revolutionary War in American history, but we are not focusing on that now." She has used _____ memory to generate the forms new to her.
 a. procedural
 b. declarative
 c. semantic
 d. episodic

37. An English language learner (ELL) student demonstrates a particular aptitude for mathematics in general, including arithmetic and algebra. The student's L1 is Arabic. The teacher incorporates vocabulary from the student's primary language into lessons in these subjects for the class and into assignments for the student. What is accurate about this practice?
 a. It is appropriate for the student's content-area abilities but is not culturally or linguistically related.
 b. It is culturally responsive and suits student content-area abilities but is not linguistically relevant.
 c. It is culturally responsive, linguistically accessible, and meets the student's content-area abilities.
 d. It is not culturally or linguistically meaningful and does not address student content-area abilities.

38. Which of the following best reflects instructional use of multicultural human resources for content-area and language learning?
 a. A teacher brings in artifacts from English language learner (ELL) students' various home countries for discussion and assigns them to write essays about what they learned.
 b. A teacher asks an EL) student's parent to present native traditions and artifacts and assigns students to write compositions about what they learned.
 c. A teacher presents a vocabulary lesson accompanied by multimedia materials that enable the students to learn by accessing different modalities.
 d. A teacher employs manipulatives to facilitate the mathematical concept understanding of younger students, both native English-speaking and ELLs.

39. A class of all English language learner (ELL) students includes two students with intellectual disabilities and three students with specific learning disabilities. Their teacher differentiates instruction to accommodate the _____ needs of these students.
 a. academic
 b. linguistic
 c. cognitive
 d. cultural

40. A high school English language learner (ELL) student at the advanced English language proficiency (ELP) level, whose career goal is to become a doctor, is applying to college and university pre-med programs. Which of the following technology tools could help this student prepare in terms of English language development (ELD) skills?
 a. Edusoft's English for Specific Purposes
 b. Pearson English Language Learning Instruction (ELLIS) digital learning program
 c. Instant Immersion's English software
 d. Lane's English as a Second Language

41. Recent research from 2014 finds that, when teachers give English language learner (ELL) students electronic instead of handwritten feedback on their written compositions

    a. the feedback was less explicit and systematic.

    b. the feedback resulted in far superior revision.

    c. the feedback did not address student needs.

    d. the feedback gave equivalent effectiveness.

42. Some refugee English language learner (ELL) students lack prior formal education and print literacy skills, yet their culture's rich oral tradition has equipped them with excellent storytelling skills, which American educators are able to use to inform their instruction in English language writing. This teaching approach, based on the assumption or view that developmental pre-reading and prewriting skills can be taught, is associated MOST with which of these underlying theories?

    a. The emergent literacy theory

    b. The interactive reading theory

    c. The funds of knowledge theory

    d. None of these

43. Among the following, which instructional approaches recently have been found MOST useful to help teenage English language learner (ELL) students who are semiliterate and nonliterate in their L1s and English?

    a. The Mutually Adaptive Learning Paradigm (MALP)

    b. The Cognitive Academic Language Learning Approach (CALLA)

    c. The framework of guided reading and running records

    d. The Sheltered Instruction Observation Protocol (SIOP)

44. What is correct related to California's English language Proficiency Level Descriptors (PLDs)?

    a. Substantial, Moderate, and Light support levels correspond to Emerging, Expanding, and Bridging.

    b. Substantial, Moderate, and Light support levels are descriptors entirely separate from the PLDs.

    c. Substantial, Moderate, and Light support levels are descriptors used within each one of the PLDs.

    d. Substantial, Moderate, and Light support levels explain how to differentiate and provide support.

45. Which of the following MOST accurately states the relationship of California English language development (ELD) and English language arts (ELA) standards in writing and how to apply them for English language learner (ELL) students?

    a. ELL students who attain ELD standards will not achieve the ELA standards as well.

    b. ELL students who attain ELA standards will automatically have met ELD standards.

    c. ELL students must achieve ELD standards before they can attempt ELA standards.

    d. ELL students can achieve either the ELD standards or ELA standards but not both.

46. An English language learner (ELL) high school senior has been assigned by the teacher to write a composition. The student decides that his target audience will be fellow students who are voting for the first time and are undecided for which candidate or party they will vote. The student further decides that his purpose will be to show this audience why one candidate is a better choice than another. Which writing genre would you expect the student to use for this composition?
   a. Narrative
   b. Expository
   c. Descriptive
   d. Persuasive

47. An English language learner (ELL) student has written this sentence: "By the times I get there they had already went to the fair without me." Among the grammatical errors included, which one occurs MOST often?
   a. Tense
   b. Number
   c. Agreement
   d. All of these

48. Which statement is MOST accurate regarding Specially Designed Academic Instruction in English (SDAIE) lesson planning for English language learner (ELL) students?
   a. The tasks with the highest complexity will always require the most scaffolding.
   b. The scaffolding amount relates to student cognitive, academic, and English language proficiency (ELP) levels.
   c. The students with the lowest English language proficiency (ELP) levels always will need the most scaffolding.
   d. The students with the highest ELP levels will always need the least scaffolding.

49. English language learner (ELL) students in one class have no previous experience with conjugating verb tenses in their native languages. What would be an effective teacher strategy to create background knowledge for this?
   a. Giving students videos of activities in past, present, and future with the corresponding words
   b. Giving students lists of verb tenses, assigning them to memorize these, and then testing them
   c. Giving students worksheets to fill in the blanks with verb tenses using sentence context clues
   d. Giving students lists of verb tenses in their native languages with English language translations

50. A teacher plans scaffolded interactions for English language learner (ELL) students by assigning them to pairs, with one partner at a higher English language proficiency (ELP) level giving peer tutoring to the other with a lower ELP level. What kind of interactions are these?
   a. Student–text
   b. Teacher–student
   c. Student–student
   d. All of these kinds

51. For a teacher of English language learner (ELL) students, including which of the following would be the MOST effective use of Specially Designed Academic Instruction in English (SDAIE) lessons?

    a. Assigning reading and writing tasks in English language development (ELD) classes and oral presentations and discussions in social studies classes

    b. Assigning reading and writing tasks in math and science classes and oral presentations and discussions in ELD classes

    c. Assigning reading and writing, oral presentations, and discussions in ELD and math, science, and social studies

    d. Assigning only reading and writing in all classes with scaffolding until students have reached higher oral English language proficiency (ELP) levels

52. An English language learner (ELL) student has grade-level listening English skills and speaks English fluently but is two grades below grade level in reading English and three grades below grade level in writing English. Which would be the MOST appropriate teacher strategy to assess this student's mastery of grade-level objectives in subject content?

    a. Use only authentic assessments.

    b. Select from multiple strategies.

    c. Scaffold all assessment tasks.

    d. Use all written assessments.

53. Of the following, which would be MOST effective to contextualize the key concepts and language in a Specially Designed Academic Instruction in English (SDAIE) lesson for English language learner (ELL) students?

    a. Provide students with English sentences that each include key subject ideas and terms.

    b. Assign students to write each key subject concept and word into full-sentence contexts.

    c. Assign students to activities using materials and resources applying key ideas and terms.

    d. Provide students glossaries in English with L1 translation of key subject ideas and terms.

54. When a teacher implements a Specially Designed Academic Instruction in English (SDAIE) lesson, which strategy would best scaffold content for English language learners (ELLs) in an accompanying assignment for a hands-on student activity?

    a. The teacher distributes print handouts of instructions for completing the assignment.

    b. The teacher gives the students instructions for completing the assignment in oral form.

    c. The teacher gives the students a demonstration modeling how to do the assignment.

    d. The teacher gives the students printed instructions and reads them aloud to students.

55. A teacher promotes autonomy in English language learner (ELL) students through debriefing. Which is correct about this strategy?

    a. Debriefing always involves reflection.

    b. Reflection always involves debriefing.

    c. Debriefing always uses text features.

    d. Debriefing is equal to self-evaluation.

56. How can teachers best communicate what they expect from English language learner (ELL) students in their English language development (ELD) and content-area performance?

    a. Give them a list of expectations in English.

    b. Give them a list of expectations in their L1.

    c. Give them a clear model of the outcomes.

    d. Give them a pretest and then a posttest.

57. A teacher has assigned English language learner (ELL) students some English-language text to read as part of a Specially Designed Academic Instruction in English (SDAIE) lesson. The teacher then asks the students to analyze and interpret the text. In what form should the teacher have them give their analyses and interpretations?
    a. In written compositions only, so they have a chance to organize and edit their ideas
    b. In oral class discussions only to avoid writing barriers and give oral language practice
    c. In both written and oral form to give equal attention to English language development (ELD) in all four of its domains
    d. In individual oral exams only to avoid embarrassment in front of the rest of the class

58. To assess English language learner (ELL) student achievement of Specially Designed Academic Instruction in English (SDAIE) lesson content, which of the following should a teacher best use?
    a. Oral assessments
    b. Written assessments
    c. Oral and written assessments
    d. Oral, written, and nonverbal assessments

59. Which of the following is a strategy important to use in Specially Designed Academic Instruction in English (SDAIE) lessons?
    a. Hands-on activities
    b. Guarded vocabulary
    c. Cooperative learning
    d. All of these

60. Among the following populations of English language learner (ELL) students, which is MOST likely to encounter cultural conflicts related to college and work as they are finishing high school?
    a. Underschooled ELL students
    b. Generation 1.5 ELL students
    c. Long-term ELL students
    d. All of these

Constructed-Response

1. In a written response, describe three strategies whereby a teacher can differentiate and scaffold assessment tasks for English language learner (ELL) students in both subject-area content and English language development (ELD). Explain how each of these strategies can evaluate both content knowledge and English language proficiency (ELP) levels.

2. Write examples of learning objectives for a lesson to instruct English language learner (ELL) students, both in English language development (ELD) and in subject-area content using Specially Designed Academic Instruction in English (SDAIE). Specify the subject area, the students' grade level, and at least two student English language proficiency (ELP) levels. State how to differentiate instruction for each level.

CTEL 3

1. Of the following elements of culture, which ones are internal or external elements?
   a. Arts and literature are internal elements.
   b. Traditional rituals and rites are external.
   c. Nonverbal communications are internal.
   d. Social roles and status are external items.

2. Which of the following perspectives or concepts can be characterized as exclusive rather than inclusive?
   a. Cultural congruence and cultural pluralism
   b. Cultural universals and cultural relativism
   c. Cultural congruence and ethnocentrism
   d. Cultural relativism and ethnocentrism

3. According to Vygotsky's sociocultural theory, teaching L2s in the zone of proximal development differs from traditional measures of language development by considering not only the student's current language development, but what else?
   a. The student's current language proficiency level
   b. What the student will be able to do in the future
   c. The student's history of language development
   d. What the student can do only if given assistance

4. Among English language learner (ELL) students, researchers find which of the following about their socioeconomic status and education levels relative to their readiness and language skills for learning English and academic content?
   a. Low-income ELLs need culturally responsive instruction more than uneducated ELLs.
   b. Uneducated ELLs need culturally responsive instruction more than low-income ELLs.
   c. Low-income ELLs are typically less educated and need culturally responsive teaching.
   d. Income and prior education levels do not affect ELL students' academic performance.

5. In studying discrimination, what did Gordon Allport propose?
   a. Favoritism for in-groups has precedence over aversion for out-groups.
   b. Favoritism for in-groups is the reason for prejudice against out-groups.
   c. Favoritism for in-groups is less powerful than hate against out-groups.
   d. He believed that (A) and (B) were both true but that (C) was not true.

6. Which of the following is MOST likely an example of cultural assimilation?
   a. A child brought to the United States at age 2 displays entirely American cultural behaviors by age 15.
   b. A child brought to the United States at age 10 displays both native and American cultural behaviors.
   c. A child brought to the United States 5 years ago is now familiar and comfortable with U.S. culture.
   d. A child brought to the United States 2 years ago has adjusted native practices to allow for new ones.

7. Four students have just arrived in the United States from other countries. Based on observable behaviors, which of them would you expect to be experiencing culture shock?
    a. The student who is excited and having a wonderful time
    b. The student who is withdrawn, silent, passive, and alone
    c. The student who is acting out aggressively in a classroom
    d. All these students

8. Among these factors influencing how much an English language learner (ELL) student becomes acculturated, which is MOST able to encompass both advantages and disadvantages within the same status?
    a. Country and culture of origin
    b. Reasons for immigrating
    c. Age upon arrival to the United States
    d. Amount of prior school

9. Regarding conflict management, which of the following conflict styles both can be used when an action or decision is needed immediately, no other choice is apparent, or nothing else works?
    a. Avoidance and confrontation
    b. Confrontation and compromise
    c. Accommodation and avoidance
    d. Avoidance and problem solving

10. A teacher gives students an activity wherein they each pick cards out of a hat with an identity (not theirs), for example, recent immigrant, refugee, learning disabled, Muslim, Jewish, Christian, poor, physically disabled, female, Deaf, human immunodeficiency virus (HIV) positive, and so on. Students complete worksheets asking three specific ways their lives, issues, and points of view will change; whether and when they will share their new identity; how they think others will treat them; whether they will be happy; and one word describing how they feel about their new identity. Then they discuss their thoughts and feelings during the activity, including which questions were harder to answer and why; which identities can be changed or chosen and which cannot; and so on. This activity helps students to develop _____ and explore _____ of various groups.
    a. empathy; stereotypes
    b. diversity; prejudices
    c. acceptance; biases
    d. identities; features

11. Which of the following is accurate regarding current immigration trends in California?
    a. California is the state that has the largest number of immigrants in the United States.
    b. California has more illegal alien immigrants than legal or naturalized citizens.
    c. California's immigrants are Latin American by majority from 2007 to 2011.
    d. California has more recent immigrants from Asia, and they are the majority.

12. The largest number of legal immigrants to California in 2012 settled in Los Angeles County. Of the following, which county had the second-largest number?
    a. San Francisco County
    b. Santa Clara County
    c. San Diego County
    d. Orange County

13. Between push and pull factors that cause people to move to America from other countries, which of the following is an example of a pull factor?
    a. Immigration by refugees from foreign wars
    b. Immigration by workers seeking better wages
    c. Immigration by people escaping terrorist regimes
    d. Immigration by subjects of political or religious exile

14. Which is MOST accurate regarding the assessment of student language skills conducted in their L2?
    a. Students usually demonstrate L2 performance equivalent to L1 norms in L2 assessment.
    b. Child–adult interactions are not influenced by cultural differences during L2 assessment.
    c. There is a risk of overidentifying students when assessing their language skills in the L2.
    d. There is a risk of under-identifying students when assessing their language skills in an L2.

15. Among strategies for assessing English language learner (ELL) children to differentiate between typical and atypical learners, which of the following is NOT a recommended consideration?
    a. Scores from a single valid, reliable instrument
    b. How long the child has been learning English
    c. The linguistic abilities of the child in English
    d. The linguistic abilities of the child in the L1

16. According to Hall's proxemics theory, which of the following is accurate?
    a. Personal and social, but not intimate, space are equivalents.
    b. Social space and public space have physically equal distances.
    c. Distance affects communication the same way among cultures.
    d. The effect of distance on communication varies across cultures.

17. Among the following nonverbal communication elements, which one is universal across cultures?
    a. Touching
    b. Gestures
    c. Eye contact
    d. None of these

18. In terms of intercultural communication, American culture is considered _____ and _____, whereas Asian cultures are considered _____ and _____.
    a. low context, analytical; high context, holistic
    b. high context, analytical; low context, holistic
    c. low context, holistic; high context, analytical
    d. high context, holistic; low context, analytical

19. Of the following, which is an effective strategy for intercultural interactions?
    a. Basing ideas about people's overall competence on a specific competence area
    b. Being honest about discomfort interacting with people from other cultures
    c. Being receptive to new or unexpected information about a culture or cultural group
    d. Being considerate not to embarrass others by overtly explaining cultural mores

20. When working to prevent and resolve cultural conflict, which of the following is NOT good advice?
    a. You can give specific feedback about certain behaviors you observed.
    b. Your first interpretation of another's behavior is most likely accurate.
    c. You can request clarification of your interpretations of the behaviors.
    d. You can give feedback about how you responded to some behaviors.

21. An elementary school teacher expecting a new English language learner (ELL) student has read that people from this student's culture are often embarrassed by being praised in front of a group, so he plans to use stickers showing approval on the student's written assignments. Which step should precede this strategy?
    a. Explaining to the student's parents the rationale for this strategy
    b. Doing extra reading about characteristics of the student's culture
    c. Asking coworkers about alternatives for positive reinforcement
    d. Finding out whether this individual student has that cultural trait

22. A physical education teacher and sports coach does not understand why an English language learner (ELL) student in her class is a great team player but shows no individual competitive spirit. This student works and plays excellently with others, always supporting his teammates, but makes no efforts to win in class exercises when classmates compete against one another. She discovers an answer after inquiring about and researching the student's home culture. What is MOST likely true about this situation?
    a. The teacher's teaching methods motivated teamwork more than competitiveness.
    b. The teacher's class has more highly competitive students than team-oriented ones.
    c. The teacher's cultural assumptions are different from the student's cultural values.
    d. The teacher's teaching style is more effective with teams than individual students.

23. A teacher wants to gain in-depth knowledge about some new English language learner (ELL) students' home cultural experiences. Of the following, which would be MOST appropriate to provide this knowledge?
    a. Having informal conversations with the students about their cultural experiences
    b. Making observations of the students' behaviors during interaction with classmates
    c. Conducting interviews with the students' parents about their cultural experiences
    d. Taking advantage of resources in the community to learn about students' cultures

24. A class has English language learner (ELL) students from Latin American, Asian, and African countries. The cultures of the students from the African countries include strong oral traditions. All students come from collectivist cultures. Which of the following learning activities would best accommodate all of their backgrounds?
    a. Assigning them to make oral presentations individually before the class
    b. Assigning them to cooperative learning groups and an oral presentation
    c. Assigning them to independent study projects and an oral presentation
    d. Assigning them to participate in a class bowl-style knowledge contest

25. Which of the following is MOST accurate regarding teacher expectations for English language learner (ELL) and native English-speaking students?
    a. Teacher expectations should be higher for ELLs because they must work harder to succeed.
    b. Teacher expectations should be higher for native English speakers because it is easier for them.
    c. Teacher expectations should be lower for ELL students because they have language barriers.
    d. Teacher expectations should be uniformly high for ELL and native English-speaking students.

26. Of the following, which teacher practice best shows respect for student linguistic diversity?
    a. Allowing English language learner (ELL) students to use their L1s and not teaching English to avoid offending them
    b. Facilitating ELLs' English language development (ELD) by permitting only English use in school
    c. Teaching ELL students ELD and allowing and validating L1 use
    d. Telling ELLs' parents to learn and speak only English at home to promote children's ELD

27. Which of these would make a school's learning environment most culturally inclusive?
    a. Presenting students with multicultural perspectives during social studies classes
    b. Having students discuss multicultural perspectives on special class culture days
    c. Assigning students to examine multicultural perspectives as enrichment projects
    d. Incorporating multicultural perspectives into all subjects in the school curriculum

28. What is a correct definition of intergroup and intragroup relations?
    a. Intergroup relations are within groups, intragroup relations among groups.
    b. Intergroup relations are among groups, intragroup relations within groups.
    c. Intergroup relations and intragroup relations are terms for the same thing.
    d. Intergroup relations and intragroup relations fit none of these definitions.

29. Regarding English language learner (ELL) parent involvement in school programs and activities, what is true?
    a. Teachers can give parents ways to help children in school via home and community visits.
    b. It is unnecessary to have union or district permission for home or community visits.
    c. Arranging for a third party to be available as an interpreter is intrusive for ELL parents.
    d. ELL parent involvement in school programs and activities should be on school grounds.

30. Which of these reflects a teaching practice that helps establish an inclusive learning environment?
    a. Ensuring consistency and equity by using a single teaching method with all students
    b. Varying learning activities, assignments, and teaching strategies for different needs
    c. Focusing on cultural diversity by devoting a special class to the study of this subject
    d. Providing students with a sense of safety through not setting rules to restrict them

31. To connect English language learner (ELL) parents with their children's educations, what is true about effective strategies?
    a. Make sure that the parents can meet with educators during normal school hours.
    b. Parents can understand collaborative, communicative school culture on their own.
    c. Meeting families' basic physical, economic, and social needs is not school business.
    d. Establish and maintain consistent communication with homes using parent liaisons.

32. Which of these is accurate about parent education classes that schools can offer to diverse families?
    a. It is not the school's place to provide information about specific disabilities.
    b. Schools should leave the prenatal care information to Planned Parenthood.
    c. Schools can provide training in effective math, reading, and similar tutoring.
    d. Only community agencies can offer information on aftercare opportunities.

33. When schools involve community members in their schools and classrooms, which of these is true about appropriately using their resources?
    a. Community members can share culture, language, and more with students and faculty.
    b. Community members can share about culture but cannot explain about languages.
    c. Community members can share cultural information but not any content expertise.
    d. Community members can share cultural information but not religion in public school.

34. A School Governance Council that includes school personnel, students, parents, and community members may include which of these in its responsibilities?
    a. Conducting school needs analyses
    b. Analyzing school achievement data
    c. Developing school improvement plans
    d. Typically, all of these duties

35. Among models of conflict management, which one incorporates all of the others?
    a. Peaceable classroom programs
    b. Curriculum infusion programs
    c. Peaceable schools programs
    d. School mediation programs

36. Which model of multicultural curriculum reform typically would involve including the Native American perspective when studying Thanksgiving traditions?
    a. The additive approach
    b. The social action approach
    c. The contributions approach
    d. The transformation approach

37. In transforming school curriculum to become multicultural, which of the following is the MOST valid principle?
    a. Teaching histories of oppression in history classes
    b. Teaching the works of underrepresented peoples
    c. Teaching multicultural concepts via single example
    d. Teaching of underrepresented peoples as unusual

38. For multicultural curriculum and instruction to be globally inclusive and locally responsive, which school activity would be optimal?
    a. A teacher who has visited a country some students come from teaches about this country.
    b. A teacher who has visited a country some students come from shares his or her experiences.
    c. A teacher who has visited a country some students come from invites their perspectives.
    d. A teacher who has visited a country some students come from does all of these together.

39. When a teacher's class includes students from collectivist cultures, which can the teacher often expect in their attitudes?
    a. Students want more opportunities to express themselves.
    b. Students are less likely to volunteer information in classes.
    c. Students are less likely to volunteer to help out classmates.
    d. Students want to achieve better grades than all classmates.

40. A student from a culture with a rich oral tradition is having difficulty starting an assignment to write an essay describing an experience. How could the teacher help by contextualizing the assignment to help access prior student knowledge?
    a. Give the student a list of key descriptive vocabulary translated from L1 to L2.
    b. Instruct the student to write the essay in L1 first and then translate it into L2.
    c. Give the student a recorder; tell him or her to dictate a story, and then write it.
    d. Instruct the student to use an earlier native language composition as a guide.

Constructed-Response

Describe one external element and one internal element of culture and how these represent cultural perspectives. Identify a significant challenge each element can involve for English language learners (ELLs), including its probable effects on their academic performance and school experience. Identify and describe a teaching strategy or strategies to address each challenge. Explain how it (or they) would be effective.

Answers and Explanations

CTEL 1

1. B: This exercise is an example of phonology, that is, learning both recognition as heard and articulation (C) as spoken of the distinctive features of individual English-language phonemes. It is not phonics (A), that is, learning to associate individual English-language phonemes with their corresponding English alphabet letters. It is not only articulation (C) when speaking but also identification when listening. It is not morphology (D), that is, learning to identify the smallest grammatically meaningful units in words, for example, a plural –s ending on a noun.

2. C: Japanese does not contain consonant clusters; consonants are commonly separated by vowels. This explains the word *sutoraiku,* which is the Japanese version of the English word *strike.* It cannot be assumed the students are generalizing this difference to all English words (A) because not all English words contain consonant clusters. Their native language does not exclude any of the consonants in the cluster (B); if it did, they would have more difficulty pronouncing those. It cannot be inferred from the example word that Japanese uses consonant clusters only in certain word positions (D) as this word contains no consonant clusters at all.

3. B: Because the first two of three objects were in infinitive form, the third also should be to maintain parallel structure. While the third object is the progressive participle of the verb used as a noun and therefore a gerund, usage of gerunds (A) is not the issue here: It would be correct to use *snowboarding* if the first two objects were *skiing, skating* rather than "to ski, skate." Similarly, use of infinitives (C) is not the problem: It was correct to use "to ski, skate," but then the third object should also be *to snowboard.* These objects are direct, not indirect (D). The only error is lack of parallelism.

4. A: The teacher needs to instruct the student about using articles before nouns. *The* is a definite article (B); *a* is an indefinite article (C). Demonstrative adjectives (D) can be used instead of articles to describe nouns, for example, *that* book or *this* desk.

5. B: Speaking a different variation (or register) of a language according to contextual influences on discourse, such as varying levels of formality and usage whether addressing equals or superiors in age and status, is an example of how discourse factors influence choices among language variations. (A) is an example of choices among different languages, not versions of the same language. (C) is an example of different learning levels between orthography and articulation, typical in English language learner (ELL) students. (D) is an example of constancy, not variation, and of regional dialectal, not stylistic, variations within a language.

6. B: Organizing and connecting ideas and unifying an essay overall through use of a thesis statement and topic sentences are elements of coherence. Cohesion (A) is more specific, involving how individual words and sentences are connected through elements like reference, pronouns, conjunctions, and repetition. Therefore, (C) and (D) are both incorrect.

7. A: Pragmatic competence in writing requires the writer to consider the purpose for writing, the intended reading audience, and other contextual factors and adjust his or her language use accordingly. These are more related to pragmatics than structure and organization (B), syntactical complexity (C), or specificity in lexical choices (D).

8. C: Expository essays try to inform or explain something, for example, a process, the advantages or disadvantages of something, a set of rules, and so on, to readers through techniques like compare and contrast, cause and effect, and so on. Narrative (A) essays tell readers a story of events or experiences from a viewpoint, commonly first person or third person. Descriptive (B) essays use vivid imagery appealing to the five senses to describe people, objects, events, or places to enable readers to envision these mentally with strong clarity and specificity. Persuasive (D) or argumentative essays try to convince readers of some position or argument, often supporting it by citing evidence from other sources and using logical reasoning.

9. B: The English words *penalty, punish,* and *penitentiary* all derive from the Latin root *pen-/poen-/puni-, (poenire, poena)*, meaning punish. *Pentagon* derives from the Greek root *pent-*, meaning five (*pente*); *peptic* from the Greek root *pept-*, meaning digest (*pessein, peptos*); and *pharmacy* from the Greek root *pharmac, (pharmakon)*, meaning drug or medicine (A). *Page, pediatric,* and *pedagogical* (C) derive from the Greek root *paed-*, meaning child (Note: The Latin root *pagin-*, meaning page, is the origin of the English nouns *pagination* and *page*, meaning a book leaf, and the verb *to page*, meaning to turn book leaves, but the origin of the noun *page*, meaning a young boy attendant or servant, and of the verb *to page*, meaning to call someone, is the Greek root *paidion*, meaning boy. *Pandemic* derives from the Greek root *pan-*, meaning all (*pas, pantos*); *phantom* from the Greek root *phan-*, meaning visible or to show (*phainein*); and *phlegm* from the Greek root *phleg-*, meaning inflammation, heat, or to burn (*phlegein*).

10. D: The English words *periscope, perimeter,* and *peripheral* all derive from the Greek root *peri*, meaning around. *Pedal, pedestrian,* and *centipede* (A) all come from the Latin root *ped– (pes, pedis)*, meaning foot. *Pending, pendulum,* and *appendage* (B) all derive from the Latin *pendere or pensare*, meaning to hang, weigh, ponder, or consider (*depend, suspend* or *suspense, pendant, pension,* and *pensive* are also from this root). *Perfectly, persistence,* and *permeate* (C) all originate from the Latin root *per*, meaning through or thoroughly.

11. A: *Cirr–* is a Greek root from *kirros*, meaning yellowish orange and is the source of the English word *cirrhosis* (liver scarring). A Latin root, *cirrus*, meaning curl, tendril, or tentacle, is the source of the English word *cirrus*, describing one type of cloud. *Cine–* (B) is from the Greek *kineō*, meaning motion, the source of the English word *cinema*. *Circ–* (C) is from the Latin *circus* or *circulus*, meaning circle or ring, the source of English words *circle, circulate,* and *circus*. *Circum–* (D) is Latin, meaning around, the source of the English words *circumference, circumlocution, circumnavigate, circumscribe,* and *circumcise*.

12. A: *Edible* and *obese* both come from the Latin *edere* and *esus*, meaning to eat and eaten. *Emetic* is from the Greek *emein* and *emetos*, meaning vomit; *emulate* is from Latin *aemulare* and *aemulus*, meaning rivaling or trying to equal (B). *Exclude* is from Latin *ex*, meaning out plus *–clud*, meaning close or shut; *exempt* is from the Latin *emptus* and *emere*, meaning buy or to buy as in *caveat emptor*, meaning "buyer beware" (C), along with *redeem* or *redemption* and *preempt*. Both words use the prefix *ex*; however, the main root of *exempt* is the *–empt* from *emptus*, which has a distinct meaning. *Ecumenical* is from the Greek *oikos*, meaning house, as are *ecology, ecological, economy, economical,* and *economics*, but *ecclesiastical* is from the Greek *ekkaleō*, meaning "I call out" or "I summon," equating to *congregation* or *assembly* in English.

13. C: Learning the Greek and Latin roots for English words is not simply a way to pass tests (A) or show off one's knowledge (B). The only English language learner (ELL) students it would enable to recognize cognates (D) are students whose native languages are Greek, Russian, Italian, French,

Spanish, or Portuguese. Other ELL students would not recognize Greek and Latin origins in English words if their L1s are not descended from Greek or Latin origins. The importance of learning roots is that, once students know their meanings, they can figure out what new vocabulary words mean from their root components. For example, knowing the Greek root *phyto* means plant, *phil(e)* means love, *poly* means many, *psych* means mind, and *soph* means wisdom allows students to decipher meanings for many unfamiliar words with these roots. Knowing the simple Latin roots *ab–* and *ad–* mean away from and toward, respectively, enables deducing meanings for a host of word prefixes; additionally, knowing Latin roots for the main parts of those words completes their meanings.

14. D: While this example may seem on the surface to indicate an ignorance of spelling (A), the misspelling actually results from an ignorance of both etymology (B) and morphology (C). Etymology is involved in that *versus* is originally a Latin word, the past participle of *vertere*, meaning to turn (and the root of a large number of other English words). Knowing its Latin origin informs its spelling, as *–us* is a more common Latin spelling (Latin words do end in *–es*, e.g., *teres*, but *–us* is far commoner). Morphology is involved in that the word *verses* is the plural of *verse*, a word originating from the same Latin root (*versus* also means turning as in a row or line of poetry) but with a different meaning and spelling. Knowing morphology informs its spelling as many English words are commonly pluralized with an *–s* ending. Knowing *versus* is not a plural but *verses* is informs the different spellings.

15. B: This student has used context clues to determine the correct meaning of the word, which is a homograph and homophone; that is, it is spelled and pronounced exactly the same way with two different meanings. Its use as a verb modified by a direct object noun, plus the additional meaning of the surrounding sentence, are context clues. This strategy did not involve apposition (A), that is, finding an appositive to define the word, for example, "Grizzly, the bear." It did not involve word structure (C) because the word is spelled and pronounced identically with either meaning. It did not involve prior L1 knowledge (D) because the question does not indicate the word or its root was familiar to the student in his or her L1.

16. D: The California State Board of Education Adopted Reading/Language Arts-English-Language Development (RLA/ELD) Programs consist of five program types: Program 1 is RLA Basic; Program 2 is RLA/ELD Basic; Program 3 is Primary Language/ELD Basic; Program 4 is Intensive Intervention RLA; and Program 5 is Intensive Intervention for English Learners (EL). All five programs are aligned with state standards (A). Only Programs 1, 2, and 3 are Basic, not all (B). Only Programs 4 and 5 are Intensive Intervention programs, not all (C). Only Program 5 specifically targets ELs, not all, so (D) is correct.

17. B: The student used *for* instead of *to*; the error was using the wrong preposition. There is no adjective (A) error. (The possessive second-person pronoun *your* is used as an adjective modifying the noun *house*, but it is used correctly.) There is no error with conjunctions (C) as there are no conjunctions in this sentence. The indirect object (D) *house* is correct.

18. C: While the text described does involve all four, the description most specifically refers to the complexity of the syntax by naming long, compound-complex sentences with multiple clauses and modifiers nested within modifiers. While complex syntax is one element of writing style (A), there are many others. While the description of the text indicates a high level of difficulty (B), the more specific reason for its difficulty level is its complex syntax. While featured language structures (D) are described, the fact that the structures featured are syntactically complex is more specific.

19. A: Including well-organized ideas and events plus a few effective details and transitional devices is one of the rubric's criteria for a score of 4. (B) is one of the criteria for a score of 3, competent communication. (C) is one of the criteria for a score of 2, developing communication. (D) names two of the criteria for a score of 1, emerging communication.

20. A: Research studies have found English language learners (ELLs) more likely to interpret native English speakers' speech literally rather than inferring figurative meanings from the contextual information provided. They have this pragmatic knowledge in their L1s but often fail to transfer it to English. Research also has found ELLs mark their L1s for politeness more than they do their English utterances, not vice versa (B). Studies show that ELLs are more sensitive to context when choosing pragmatic strategies in their L1s than in English, not vice versa (C). Researchers have also found ELLs more likely to underemphasize context factors like social power and social distance when choosing pragmatic strategies in English, not to exaggerate these (D).

21. C: The question on speech functions is part of the kindergarten (K) through Grade 12 Speaking assessment of the California English Language Development Tests (CELDTs). This item addresses phonological production by assessing student speech for communicating basic needs. Choose and give reasons (A) is also one of the questions on each (K–2, 3–5, 6–8, and 9–12) of the K through Grade 12 Speaking tests, but it assesses participation in social conversations by asking and answering questions, including critical thinking skills for choosing between two options and logically explaining the choice with relevant reasons as well as assessing spoken pronunciation, vocabulary, and grammar. The highest scores allow errors not affecting communication. Hence, this item does include phonological production, but that is not the predominant factor tested as it is in Speech Functions. Short Compositions (B) is an item on the Grades 2 through 12 Writing test, which does not involve phonological production. Copying Letters (D) is an item on the K through Grade 2 Writing test.

22. A: This exercise applies syntactic clues to determine semantics, that is, (1) the use of negation and (2) the use of different word order in the second and third sentences to impart different meanings. It does not use meaning to determine sentence structure (B) because the sentence structures were already given, and the students had to use them to understand meaning and resolve ambiguities. It did not use sentence structure and meaning to determine grammar (C), which also already was established and the students did not specifically analyze. The exercise did not use sentence structure and meaning to determine vocabulary (D): They did not encounter any new or unfamiliar words in these sentences.

23. D: Choose and give reasons, an item in the kindergarten through Grade 12 Speaking tests, corresponds to the English Language Development (ELD) standard: "Actively participate in social conversations with peers and adults on familiar topics by asking and answering questions and soliciting information." This tests the social functions of language. Word analysis (A), an item in the Reading tests, corresponds to the ELD standard: "Apply knowledge of word relationships, such as roots and affixes, to derive meaning from literature and texts in content areas." This tests how students apply morphology knowledge to understand what they read. 4-Picture narrative (B), an item in the Speaking tests, corresponds to the ELD standard: "Make oneself understood when speaking by using consistent Standard English grammatical forms, sounds, intonation, pitch, and modulation but may make random errors." This tests academic functions of language more than social functions. Reading comprehension (C), an item in the Reading tests, corresponds to the ELD standard: "Read text and use detailed sentences to explain orally the main idea and details of informational text, literary text, and text in content areas." This tests ability to read and understand written and print English, not the social functions of spoken English.

24. B: The significant distinction in this example is a difference between written and spoken English in that the words given are spelled identically in written English but pronounced differently in spoken English. Therefore, English language learner (ELL) students can more easily understand meaning when hearing these words spoken, but when reading written English, they may need to use context clues to determine which part of speech and meaning the word has. While these examples all stress the first syllables of nouns and the second syllables of verbs (A), the difference between nouns and verbs is not the most significant aspect as (1) not all English nouns and verbs with common roots and meanings are spelled identically, and (2) the distinctive element is that spoken and written English do not equally indicate different meanings of these words. These words do not have different orthographies (C); they are identical orthographically but differ in pronunciation. The respective spellings and pronunciations in each pair are not similar (D) but different.

25. B: In terms of pragmatics, for the students to learn how to engage in oral discourse appropriate to different contexts, purposes, and audiences, the teacher assigns not only presentations on academic subjects but also on personal subjects that incorporate humor and use more informal registers. The former helped them learn oral discourse for the purpose of informing, explaining, describing, and persuading; the latter helps them learn oral discourse for the purpose of amusing and entertaining. The former suits school and future professional contexts; the latter suits school, social, and leisure contexts. The former suits scholastic peer and adult audiences; the latter suits school, social, leisure, peer, and adult audiences. Getting students to loosen up (A), helping them fit in and be more popular (C), and giving them a break from academic English (D) might be by-products of this assignment, but they are not its purpose. The object is to develop versatility in discourse.

26. B: Chomsky is the best known among nativist language acquisition theorists. He has proposed that we all have an inborn Language Acquisition Device (LAD), an innate universal grammar, and the ability to generate transformations enabling an unlimited number of combinations. Skinner (A) was a famous behaviorist who proposed that language acquisition is explained by the principles of operant conditioning, that is, the antecedents and consequences (events preceding and following) behaviors that control them, including verbal behaviors. Vygotsky (C), who proposed a sociocultural theory of learning, subscribed to the social interactionist interpretation of language acquisition, as has Robin Chapman (D) in proposing the Child Talk model of language development.

27. B: Being able to classify different parts of speech according to their functions (e.g., a noun is a person, place, or thing; a verb is an action or state of being or mind; adjectives describe nouns; adverbs describe verbs, adjectives, and other adverbs, etc.) demonstrates the cognitive process of categorization—sorting things into different groups sharing common characteristics. Memorization (A) is demonstrated more by remembering vocabulary words and their definitions, for example. Generalization (C) is demonstrated more by applying a rule to all or most specific instances; for example, all regular nouns are pluralized by adding –s, or all regular verbs are made past tense by adding –ed, and so on. Metacognition (D), or thinking about thinking, is demonstrated by processes like analyzing one's own patterns of grammatical or spelling errors, one's own writing style, and so on.

28. A: One similarity between first- and second-language acquisition is that learners of all ages go through the same learning sequences and stages whether they are learning a first or second language. Another similarity is that receptive learning precedes expressive learning in both L1 and L2; this does not differ (B). Learners undergo a silent period with first and second languages.

Another similarity is that learners of all ages may overgeneralize vocabulary or grammatical rules in either language; this does not depend on age or language (C). One difference between L1 and L2 acquisition is that learners have universal grammar as their only basis of acquisition, whereas when learning a second language, they additionally have their L1 as a learning basis (D).

29. A: Krashen defines acquisition as the unconscious, natural process whereby children learn their first language, focusing on the act of communication through meaningful interactions. Hence (B) and (C) are incorrect. Krashen defines learning as a conscious process, which is the result of formal instruction about a language, for example, learning the rules of its grammar. He finds acquisition more important and natural than learning (D).

30. A: Krashen's theory includes five major hypotheses: the Acquisition-Learning hypothesis; the Monitor hypothesis; the Input hypothesis; the Natural Order hypothesis; and the Affective Filter hypothesis. The Monitor hypothesis involves both acquisition and learning by defining how learning influences acquisition and explaining their relationship. While acquisition systems initiate utterances, learning systems monitor them. The Input hypothesis does not involve both (B), only acquisition but not learning. Comprehensible input, which promotes L2 progress and improvement, is within the learner's receptive comprehension but one step past the learner's current stage of expressive competence. The Natural Order hypothesis cites research evidence that learning of grammatical structures follows a natural, predictable order. However, Krashen says L2 instruction should not be dictated by this hypothesis (C); moreover, he says grammar instruction should not be sequenced at all for language acquisition goals. His Affective Filter hypothesis means negative affect can interfere with L2 acquisition, and positive affect is required but is not enough by itself (D).

31. C: While Krashen hypothesizes that conscious learning serves the function of a monitor in L2 performance, he finds this role is or should be minor, used only to polish L2 speech and correct errors. Three conditions he says are necessary for the learning system to act as monitor are that the learner has enough time (A); the learner thinks about or focuses on correct form (B); and the learner knows the language rule involved (D).

32. B: This is an example of the strategy of elaboration: After his classmate did not understand his English utterance, Sami explained he had translated a common expression from his L1 into English and further explained what it meant. Repetition (A) is a cognitive strategy English language learners (ELLs) may use to practice and commit to memory new vocabulary words, grammatical rules, spelling rules, syntactical structures, and so on. Self-monitoring (C) is a cognitive strategy of paying attention to and revising one's utterances to be more understandable to others; Sami did not use this strategy during his initial utterance. This is not an example of formulaic expressions (D): Though the saying Sami was thinking of may have been formulaic in his L1, his translation of it was not formulaic in English.

33. A: This is an example of teacher code-switching for the purpose of informing the student's L2 learning with his previous L1 learning experience. Teachers and students both use code-switching for various reasons. Role-playing for real-life L2 practice (B) would be demonstrated by practicing how to complete various real-life transactions in English through authentic simulations, for example, making restaurant reservations by phone, negotiating a car purchase, and so on. Requesting clarification (C) would be if either the teacher or student asked for additional explanation or elaboration of a communication he or she did not understand. Appealing for assistance (D), if applied to this example, would be done by the student, not the teacher; it involves asking for help with communicating something in the L2.

34. C: English language learner (ELL) students who develop their receptive skills for listening and reading in English typically find it easier to speak and write in English. L2 acquisition follows the same sequence as L1 acquisition in that learners gain receptive understanding before they gain expressive production; the former informs the latter.

35. B: Basic Interpersonal Communication Skills (BICS) are needed by English language learner (ELL) students for social communication during every day interpersonal interactions. ELL students typically acquire BICS in English about six months to two years after coming to America, of necessity and because these skills are not that cognitively demanding. However, students can take five to seven years to develop Cognitive Academic Language Proficiency (CALP) (B). If they have no previous education or no L1 development support, they can take 7 to 10 years to catch up with peers. ELL students need BICS for social purposes (A) and CALP for academic reasons (C). School administrators and teachers should not assume that ELL students are proficient in English based solely on good BICS (D) as good social English does not necessarily mean they are equipped to succeed academically using English.

36. D: On the California English Language Development Tests (CELDTs) Writing test for Grades 3 through 5, the Short Compositions question uses the following scores: 0 = no communication; 1 = emerging communication (A); 2 = developing communication (B); 3 = competent communication (D); and 4 = fully competent communication (C).

37. A: This example illustrates cognitive styles. Some students have predominantly visual learning styles; some, like this student, have predominantly auditory; some have haptic or kinesthetic learning styles, and so on. This example does not illustrate language transfer (B): The student is described as discriminating between L1 and L2, not reproducing features of L1 in L2. It does not illustrate previous knowledge (C): Nothing is mentioned about what the student knew before learning the L2. It does not illustrate physiological factors (D): Though this student likely has good hearing to have such strong auditory orientation, the orientation is described, not hearing acuity.

38. D: This example describes the pedagogical process of scaffolding: providing support for tasks students cannot perform unassisted and then gradually withdrawing that support as they gain more proficiency until they can perform the tasks independently. Assessing language proficiency (A) would entail testing student language development levels and the L2 language elements they do and do not know and can or cannot use. Providing constructive feedback (B) would involve telling students about language aspects they have performed well, those they can improve on, and techniques and strategies they can use to improve them. Building on student L1 knowledge (C) would involve relating, comparing, or translating things they know in their L1s to analogous or similar things in the L2.

39. B: Both English language learner (ELL) and native English-speaking students receive correction only to a small percentage of their most major language errors in real-world, natural situations. The classroom should approximate natural settings to make English language learning as similar as possible to what students will encounter in real life. Correcting every single error immediately and explicitly (A) can interrupt communicative flow, damage student self-esteem, and decrease student motivation. The same is true for focusing correction on students by error quantity and quality (C). Ignoring errors caused by L1 interference (D) is an arbitrary choice; the criterion for correction should be whether an error significantly interferes with meaning. Implicitly correcting only such errors is most effective for promoting ELLs' fluent English speech.

40. C: Including English language learner (ELL) students' native languages and cultures in school instruction and activities affirms their linguistic and cultural identities, enhancing self-esteem. This inclusive learning environment promotes their English language development. Tactics that attempt to restrict (A), direct (B), or accelerate (D) activities to only English language and mainstream American culture deny or denigrate students' and families' original languages and cultures, damaging their self-esteem and identities. Thus, these are not effective. Attempting to force adoption of language and culture produces aversion instead and is an undemocratic approach.

41. A: Although some educators have believed it counterproductive when children learn two languages simultaneously (B), others have said that it would confuse students to learn a new language after the age of basic L1 mastery (C), and still others believe that learning more than one language would impede the rate of development in both languages, whether simultaneous or sequential (D). Research studies find that not only does bilingual language learning not interfere with development in either language, but moreover, it can confer benefits (A) such as greater cognitive flexibility, more comfort with new learning content and experiences, larger vocabulary development when the two languages have cognates or similar roots, better facility for learning additional new languages, and superior overall linguistic competence.

42. D: When English language learner (ELL) students use code-switching for reiteration (A), they say something in English and then repeat it in their L1 to clarify understanding—either because they did not translate it into English exactly or to show the teacher they understand instructional content. Code-switching for equivalence (B) occurs when a student does not know the correct English word for a meaning and says it in the L1 instead to supply that meaning without interrupting communication. Similarly, when an ELL student does not know or cannot recall an English word, he or she may code-switch for a floor holding (C) function—to prevent communication gaps during English conversations. When the student's native language and English do not have culturally equivalent words for a meaning, an ELL student may use code-switching for conflict control (D), to prevent misunderstanding (e.g., Americans have adopted the Spanish words *machismo* and *macho* directly into our lexicon because our culture had no comparable English words for the meaning).

43. C: This example demonstrates the role of prior student knowledge in L2 development: With idioms, it is more difficult to explain a figurative meaning in English when the actual words make no literal sense. Instead, the (fortunately) multilingual teacher supplies each student with equally idiomatic expressions in their L1s having the equivalent meaning, accessing the students' prior knowledge. This is not an example of negative language transfer (A) but positive transfer: Both L1s have their own idioms with the same meaning as the English idiom, so L1s inform L2 meaning. This is much less a matter of language proficiency level (B): Idioms are the most difficult forms for even advanced English language learner (ELL) students, often requiring direct experience and contextual clues (e.g., if the teacher were not multilingual). This example does not involve cognitive or learning styles (D).

44. A: Excepting children raised bilingually, L2 learners are more often older than L1 learners. Being older, they derive more benefit from having developed more metacognition whereby they can analyze, understand, describe, explain, and manipulate linguistic and grammatical structures, which can enable them to learn faster. Age affects proficiency in both L1 and L2 learning (B). Universal grammar influences younger L1 learners more than older L2 learners (C), who are more likely to have less access to it as they have already mastered their L1s in earlier childhood. Older L2 learners are also less likely to be as sensitive to phonological features in an L2 that their L1 does not include (D).

45. C: Normally, L1 learners always achieve native proficiency in their own languages (B) except when they have disabilities that affect language learning (C). Conversely, L2 learners are not as likely to achieve native-like proficiency in the L2 as L1 learners are (A). Reasons for this include that L2 learners typically do not have as many chances as L1 learners for authentic language learning and practice (D) with native speakers: L1 learners typically learn in real-life settings, whereas L2 learners typically learn in classrooms; and L1 learners typically have many more opportunities to practice with parents, caregivers, and family members, whereas L2 learners may have more limited access to practice with native English speakers.

46. B: The Grades 2 through 12 California English Language Development Tests (CELDTs) performance descriptors say that at the beginning (A) proficiency level, "Frequent errors make communication difficult." At the early intermediate (D) level, the descriptor says, "Frequent errors still reduce communication." At the intermediate (B) level, the descriptor says, "Errors still complicate communication." At the early advanced (C) level, the descriptor says, "Errors are less frequent and rarely complicate communication." (At the advanced level, the descriptor says, "Errors are infrequent and do not reduce communication.")

47. D: Receptive language learning precedes and informs expressive language development in both L1s and L2s. Hence, English language learner (ELL) students should develop some English reading proficiency to help them succeed in writing English rather than simply beginning to write without any previous English reading experience (A). While speaking English (B) will undoubtedly help their overall English language proficiency, it will not inform English writing as well as reading English will. Listening to spoken English (C) will inform speaking better than writing in English.

48. C: Basic Interpersonal Communication Skills (BICS) is the form of English needed for English language learners (ELLs) to communicate socially on an everyday basis with peers, teachers, administrators, and so on. A student feeling isolated by an inability to communicate with peers in English needs BICS. A student functioning well socially in English already (A) has BICS; for a calculus course, this student needs Cognitive Academic Language Proficiency (CALP) to understand and correctly use the extensive technical terminology specific to the mathematical subject of calculus. A student who needs to learn how to have English conversations (C) needs BICS, not CALP. In a social studies seminar that requires 100% discussion (D), an ELL student needs BICS more than CALP in order to participate in class-length discussions. While there will be some social studies terminology, it will not be as highly technical and extensive as in calculus. The amount of interpersonal communication required in the seminar will require good BICS more.

49. A: Validating the student's native culture and language is found to raise self-esteem in English language learner (ELL) students, making it easier for them to acclimate and learn English. Conversely, directing the focus onto mainstream culture and language (B) implies the teacher does not value or appreciate the student's home culture and language, which would lower self-esteem and impede English language development. Experts also advise teachers not to lower academic expectations (C) for students from diverse backgrounds, including those with different cultures and languages as well as those with disabilities. Academic expectations should be realistic yet equally rigorous for all students. Teachers should provide students with ample supportive and constructive feedback rather than exclusively corrective feedback (D), which again lowers self-esteem and interferes with learning.

50. C: India was originally a British colony like America but for more than 400 years. Today, India regards English as both an international language and a key language, hence Indian schools

routinely teach English along with other languages. Nakul is more likely to be English proficient, having attended school since age three. Javier's family fled a terrorist regime in Honduras, hence he is more likely circumstantially bilingual, whereas Nakul and his family are more likely electively bilingual (A). Though Spanish is much more similar to English in alphabet, vocabulary, and pronunciation than Indian languages, the history of English instruction in the two countries is more germane to each student's English proficiency (B). Given the lower likelihood of English education in a Honduran terrorist regime and higher likelihood of circumstantial bilingualism, Javier is less likely than Nakul to be as motivated to speak English and be proficient in doing so; Nakul's likelier long familiarity with English and family's probable elective bilingualism make his English-speaking motivation and proficiency more likely (D).

CTEL 2

1. B: Backward Design, Stage 1—Desired Results includes essential knowledge and skills the students will understand (A) under Understandings, and, under Established Goals, which learning, program, or course objectives or content standards will be met by the design (C). Stage 2—Assessment Evidence includes which authentic performance tasks will be used for students to demonstrate their understandings and which criteria will be used to judge these (B). Stage 3—Learning Plan includes which instruction, learning activities, and experiences will help students achieve the targeted results (D).

2. D: Using a variety of instructional modalities relates most to offering English language learners (ELLs) multiple learning opportunities. (A) relates more to using multiple measures for assessing ELL performance. (B) and (C) both relate more to creating an appropriate testing environment. These are all strategies for differentiating standards-based instruction and assessment for ELL, but (D) relate most to providing varied instructional modalities, while the others relate to assessment variety and environment.

3. A: A summative assessment is best for evaluating whether students have attained the state standards that the instruction was designed to meet. Valuating students' progress during instruction (B), determining how to modify instruction to make it more effective (C), and designing further differentiated, standards-based instruction for given students (D) are all more appropriately evaluated by using formative assessments.

4. C: After the California English language arts (ELA) standards were developed for all students, it became apparent that many English language learner (ELL) students entering American schools with lower levels of English language proficiency (ELP) would be unable to attain the standards' rigorous benchmarks at their own grade levels. Therefore, English language development (ELD) standards were developed after, not before, ELA standards (A) to support and assess ELL students' progress toward meeting ELA standards. The two are not similar at every proficiency level (B); however, they are quite similar at the advanced level (C), when ELL students are expected to have attained native-like English proficiency. At the same time, the two are not completely different at all levels (D) because the ELD standards are designed to help ELL students acquire the ELA standards over time and thus are compatible with them.

5. A: Backward Design differs from other instructional planning processes in that teachers have to plan a variety of assessments before they plan learning activities; they do not develop both at the same time (B); they do not plan lessons before assessments, and the authors advise assessment throughout the learning sequence, not only at its end (D). While they emphasize authentic

performance tasks, the authors recommend balancing these with tests, quizzes, observation, and other more traditional assessments rather than replacing the latter with the former (C).

6. B: This is an issue of test reliability, which is the ability of a test to yield the same or similar results across repeated administrations to the same test takers. Validity (A) is the ability of a test to measure what it claims and intends to measure. While the varying reliability of the test described between native English-speaking versus English language learner (ELL) students is likely due to test bias (C) in favor of the former and to the latter's detriment; still the fact that it does not obtain similar results across repeated administrations with the same ELL students makes it primarily an issue of reliability. Therefore, (D) is incorrect.

7. A: The excessive number of idiomatic expressions is an example of test bias: Only native English-speaking students would understand these. The test would only be unreliable (B) if it did not get the same or similar results across repeated administrations to the same students. It would be invalid (C) only if it did not test what it claimed or meant to test. It did not reveal a weakness of the ELLs (D): Idioms are known to be more difficult than other language features for foreign learners because they often do not make literal sense and require familiarity with each expression for understanding (unless their L1s have similar idioms they are informed of for comparison). Given enough contextual information, some ELLs can figure out what idioms mean but, without knowing their origins, often cannot see or remember the connection between words and meaning.

8. C: This California English language development (CELD) standard is the reference for an item under the category of Teacher Talk on the kindergarten through Grade 2 (K–2) Listening test of the California English Language Development Tests (CELDTs). (It is also referenced under the Extended Listening Comprehension category.) The category of Following Oral Directions (A) on the K–2 Listening test references this standard: "Respond to simple directions and questions by using physical actions and other means of nonverbal communication (e.g., matching objects, pointing to an answer, drawing pictures)." The category of Oral Vocabulary (B) on the K–2 Speaking test references this standard: "Begin to speak a few words or sentences by using some English phonemes and rudimentary English grammatical forms (e.g., single words or phrases)." The category of Rhyming (D) on the K–2 Listening test references this standard: "Answer simple questions with one- to two-word responses."

9. C: The English language arts (ELA) part of the California High School Exit Examination (CAHSEE) is aligned with California academic content standards through Grade 10, not 12 (A). It includes multiple-choice questions in the reading portion and a writing task in the writing portion, not essay questions in both (B). The reading portion covers vocabulary, reading comprehension, analysis of informational texts, and analysis of literary texts (C). The writing task requires a written response to literature, an informational passage, or a writing prompt, not literature only (D).

10. A: One criterion used for releasing questions from past editions of the California Standards Test (CST) is that they cover enough of the academic content standards that the corresponding grade's English language arts (ELA) test evaluates. Another criterion is that the questions selected to release demonstrate a range, not uniformity (B) of difficulty levels. A third criterion is that the questions represent various, not uniform (C) ways of testing the standards. Once questions from past CST exams are released, none of these is ever reused on any future tests (D).

11. C: The strategy that the teacher can implement immediately, easily, and effectively is to differentiate the levels of questions he or she asks for class discussion to check whether every student understands the material and to what extent. Asking the district to provide alternative

benchmarks for English language learner (ELL) students (A) cannot be implemented immediately or easily and is not likely to happen as district officials rightly will want all students to meet the same benchmarks and state standards; other mechanisms are already in place, for example, in California, English language development (ELD) standards designed to help and assess ELL progress toward eventually meeting state English language arts (ELA) standards for all students. Requesting alternative textbooks with easier assessments (B) also cannot be implemented immediately or easily: Books cost money; the class already has one set of texts, and the district will not want to vary them for the same reasons as (A). Of course, the teacher should also differentiate instructional levels for ELLs (D), but this is an incorrect answer because the question is about the most appropriate strategy specifically for assessment, not instruction.

12. B: Indicating one picture among several to answer questions is a way that English language learners (ELLs) at beginning proficiency levels can show their content knowledge and their receptive (listening) understanding of English (A) without being penalized by having inadequate expressive (speaking) English skills interfere (C); these are advantages. Because picture selection is a receptive response mode, there is no risk they will communicate incorrect or unclear meanings through incorrect word choice (D), another advantage. Hence the only listed limitation of this response method is that, by responding without speaking, students have no way to elaborate upon or explain their responses further (B).

13. B: The Student Study Team (SST) (A) would determine if student school difficulties were caused by learning disabilities; medical, physical, psychological, social, or other problems; or language barriers. It is already known this student knows no English, and the specialist has identified very high IQ and adaptive functioning in his L1 but no disabilities. Hence, a special education (C) referral or other intervention programs (D) are not indicated. A Gifted and talented education (GATE) (B) referral is indicated because this student's IQ and other scores show he is intellectually and adaptively gifted or talented.

14. D: An English language learner (ELL) student with visual impairment would benefit from more listening and oral assignments instead of more read and written work, not vice versa. Differentiated instruction appropriate to the student's language level (A) will address student ELL needs. Preferential front-of-room seating (B) will address the visual impairment; so will providing magnifiers, large-print text, and audio recordings (C).

15. A: Giving English language learner (ELL) students a glossary of English chemistry terms to write experiment reports is an example of scaffolding a content-area assessment task. (B), (C), and (D) are all examples of scaffolding English language development (ELD) assessment tasks for ELL students.

16. D: Meeting the California state content standards for the core curriculum, including English language arts (ELA) as well as all other subjects, is the definitive goal of English language learner (ELL) education programs in California. Hence, at all grade levels, ELL programs must provide both access to core curriculum content and English language development (ELD).

17. D: Researchers conducting studies investigating various public school districts and systems have documented that some gifted English language learner (ELL) students have not been placed in gifted education programs due to language barriers (A); some ELL students without disabilities have been incorrectly placed in special education programs due to language barriers (B); and some schools have systematically placed ELL students in classrooms with less-qualified teachers (C) as well as many other educational equity issues.

18. D: By virtue of having had more formal education in her home country and having tested at the same English language proficiency (ELP) level on the California English Language Development Tests (CELDTs) for three years, Student B can handle more rigorous writing instruction to reach grade level this year. Although Student A is two years behind grade level, this does not mean she should also reach grade level within one school year (A) or advance two years in writing English language proficiency (ELP) level within that time (C). The fact that her writing ELP advanced one year on last year's ELDT does not necessarily mean she will find it easier to move up another level this year (B). Student B's longer time at her current ELP level in writing, along with her longer formal schooling and being one year less behind grade level, may very well make it easier for her to advance to grade level this year.

19. A: The third grader whose English language development (ELD) level is early intermediate should be placed in content-based ELD because of the student's lower grade level, lower English language proficiency (ELP), more time to learn academic content, and need to improve ELP now before academic content becomes more difficult. The seventh grader (B) and tenth grader (C) should be placed in Specially Designed Academic Instruction in English (SDAIE) because of their higher grade levels, intermediate levels of ELP, and below or far below basic educational levels relative to their grade levels to receive more instruction in academic content areas as they have comparatively less time to learn this content. Therefore (D) is incorrect.

20. C: Because the teacher is bilingual in the parents' native language, a bilingual phone call or home visit would be most effective and appropriate to communicate their rights to them. Because the parents speak little or no English, mailing English-language documents (A) or e-mailing a summary in English (B) would be ineffective and inappropriate. Because the parents have no formal education in their native language, mailing or e-mailing written information (D) would be less effective and appropriate than oral communication, which they could understand better.

21. B: Because these students had months of conversational English experience before starting school, listening to audio recordings of books being read aloud as they read them will access their English listening skills to inform and support developing their English reading skills. Vocabulary lists with translations (A) will facilitate L1–L2 vocabulary transfer but not access their English listening skills. Side-by-side English and L1 translated text (C) will facilitate L1–L2 reading transfer but not use English listening skills for English reading. Paired reading assignments (D) would help only if their partners were native English-speaking students or English language learner (ELL) students with higher levels of English reading proficiency; however, pairing within this same group of students would not: None knows any more about written English, and in even trying to help each other with reading comprehension, they would be more likely to converse in their L1 than in English.

22. A: This most illustrates motivation: This student had a very social nature and was used to and liked having many friends. This motivated him to develop conversational English skills quickly to make new friends. This does not illustrate vocabulary knowledge (B) as his primary motivation was not to learn as many new English words as quickly as possible but to learn whatever English words and structures he needed for social conversation. While his background experiences (C) of having many friends were related to and influenced his learning, those experiences themselves were also a function of his social nature and motivation to have friends. The same motivation to make new friends in a new country is illustrated more by this example than the fact that he had many friends before. This example does not illustrate the student's English language proficiency level (ELP) (D); rather, it illustrates which personal factor influenced his development of that proficiency level and

in which area (social rather than academic). The student was comparatively less motivated to develop academic English literacy than social conversational English.

23. D: Marzano's six steps are (1) teacher explanations, descriptions, or examples of the words; (2) linguistic definition (C)—students paraphrase the teacher's explanations, descriptions, or examples using their own words; (3) nonlinguistic definition (D)—students create pictures, pictographs, symbolic representations of the words, or they act them out; (4) activities—teachers engage students in activities that enhance their understanding of the words' meanings; (5) discussion (B)—teachers ask students periodically to discuss the words with each other; and (6) games (A)—teachers provide games for students to play that involve the words and reinforce their knowledge of them.

24. C: Graphic organizers are visual representations of concepts, words, or other learning matter. As such, they help English language learner (ELL) students, students with reading-related learning disabilities, students with cognitive deficits, and others who may have difficulty accessing verbal information. Learning logs (A) typically use written language and hence are verbal or linguistic in nature. Shared reading (B) requires students to read written language together with peers or others, and thus is linguistic in nature. Interactive journals (D) allow students to think independently and creatively, process classroom information, and express their own ideas. While these typically include pictures and other nonlinguistic elements, they typically also involve writing and include words. Hence, of these choices, graphic organizers are typically the most visual and nonlinguistic.

25. A: Role, audience, format, topic (RAFT) is a post-reading strategy that can be applied flexibly to support students in responding in writing to reflect about and analyze their reading. The teacher or class makes suggestions, from which students select a role to play, an audience to address, a format to use, and a topic to cover in writing about what they have read. The question–answer relationships (QAR) (B) strategy is used before, during, and after reading to help students identify the four question–answer relationships most common in the texts they will read—"Right There," "Think and Search," "Author and You," and "On My Own" questions—and answer these about the text. Questions only (C) is used before, during, and after reading as a strategy to teach students how to ask questions about the text and read actively to answer them. The reader's–writer's notebook (D) is a strategy used before, during, and after reading for students to have conversations with and about text, connecting their own thoughts, background, prior knowledge, opinions, and biases to the reading to build comprehension.

26. A: The references to sensory details, modifiers, and wording in this learning objective identify it as representing the English component of the interdisciplinary unit. The references to antibodies and response to infection in (B) identify this objective as representing the biology component of the unit. The references to influences on substance use in (C) identify this objective as representing the health component of the unit. Therefore, (D) is incorrect.

27. C: The Benchmark Group is defined by the California Reading and Language Arts (RLA) framework as "generally making good progress toward the standards but may be experiencing temporary or minor difficulties." It is stressed that while not "critical," these needs must be met promptly to prevent students falling behind. The Strategic Group (A) is defined as one to two standard deviations below the mean on standardized tests, yet "their learning difficulties, which must be examined with systematic and, occasionally, intensive and concentrated care, can often be addressed by the regular classroom teacher with minimal assistance within the classroom environment." The Intensive Group (B) is defined as "seriously at risk," having "extremely and

chronically low performance on one or more measures. . . . These students perform well below the mean." The framework recommends a student success team (SST) referral and suggests special education referral in some cases. The framework does not list a special needs group (D) along with the other three but does include guidelines to develop effective teaching strategies "for all students" that incorporate planning for students with special needs. These guidelines immediately follow the three group descriptions.

28. D: Objective (A) addresses only content standards for social studies. Objective (B) addresses only English language development (ELD) standards for social studies. Objective (C) adds "in written English" but still addresses only ELD standards for social studies. Objective (D) includes both content standards, that is, explaining social studies concepts, and ELD standards, that is, explaining economics vocabulary terms plus explaining both in written English for social studies.

29. B: With a number of English language learner (ELL) students within the mainstream English language classroom including three different levels of English language proficiency (ELP), peer tutoring is a natural choice to support their learning. The students at higher ELP levels can tutor those at lower levels. Technology (A) is a significant support to supplement teacher instruction and facilitate all kinds of student activities. Its inclusion will not detract from, and may be incorporated in, peer tutoring. However, using technologies instead of peer tutoring is not as obvious a choice to support ELLs at varying ELP levels as peer tutoring. Team teaching (C) can be very effective but, in this case, may not be needed if ELLs can help and be helped by their ELL peers. Paraprofessionals (D) who are bilingual can help ELLs, especially those with lower ELP; however, in this case, ELL peers can serve the same function.

30. D: One way to reach out to parents lacking English language skills is informing them of learning opportunities in the community they can pursue, of which they may not know, including English and native language literacy courses, parenting courses, family literacy projects, and so on. Teachers can ask school administrators to research, compile, and regularly update lists of such resources, available in both English and parents' native languages. Learning even a few common words and phrases in the parents' language does much good (A) by making them feel welcome and showing the teacher is making the effort to communicate. Teachers should find fully bilingual adult interpreters rather than use the student (B), which can make parents feel disempowered. Monolingual teachers can give parents contact information for bilingual staff members. This is not passing parents off (C) but providing them with additional resource people to discuss educational issues in their language. Teachers also can give parents contacts for other parents speaking their language to help each other and share their experiences. Asking parents able and willing to volunteer is also beneficial.

31. D: Cummins' model goes vertically bottom to top from cognitively undemanding to cognitively challenging and horizontally, left-to-right, from high-context (personally relevant to students) to abstract. Hence, quadrant A (A) is at bottom left and represents tasks and activities that are not intellectually hard and to which students can relate personally. Quadrant B (B) is at top left and represents tasks and activities that are relevant to students but more cognitively demanding. Quadrant C (C) is at top right and represents tasks and activities that are abstract or hard for students to relate to personally and are also cognitively difficult. Quadrant D (D) is at bottom right and represents tasks and activities that are abstract but cognitively easy. Therefore, easy but abstract or irrelevant tasks would be found in quadrant D.

32. D: Realia (A) and manipulatives (C) are both concrete, hands-on objects and materials, which younger children can access and understand more easily. Kindergarten through Grade 1 students

will have more difficulty comprehending concepts unless they are accompanied by concrete objects they can see, touch, and manipulate. Analogies (B), that is, comparing one concept to another, are too abstract for children at these ages as they do not provide anything concrete to help them understand the abstract ideas involved.

33. C: This represents the evaluative level of meaning at which the reader analyzes and makes judgments, conclusions, and generalizations about the text and its larger implications. Specifically, the student has decided that the ending described by the author is not credible based on the rest of the story. A response to this ending at the literal (A) level of meaning might be, "After the end of this story, all of the characters in it went on to have happy lives." A response at the inferential (B) level might be, "After this story ended, none of the characters in it had any more problems like the ones they had during the story." The student would be inferring by predicting probable subsequent outcomes. Because (C) is correct, (D) is incorrect.

34. A: The teacher should use simple sentence structures for these students instead of compound, complex, or compound-complex sentence structures. The teacher need not use simpler word choices (B) because these students have developed English language vocabulary at grade-level difficulty. Neither does the teacher need to use a smaller range of words (C) for the same reason; the students know an equal number of grade-level vocabulary words as native English-speaking classmates. The teacher needs only to vary the sentence structure of questions but not the choice of words in them (D).

35. B: The teaching practice described will help English language learner (ELL) students with comprehension and memory for new English words by giving them a learning strategy of categorizing words by their characteristics of structure and meaning. The teacher has taught them a cognitive tool they can use in various academic contexts and independently build their subject content and English language proficiency (ELP). Syntactic and semantic word classification is unrelated to differentiating main and supporting ideas (A) in reading or writing (or listening or speaking). Grouping words in categories will not help the students plan or organize compositions (C); it will only help them remember and retrieve the most appropriate words for compositions. While reducing performance anxiety with English tasks (D) may be a by-product of improved English word comprehension and retention, it is not the main purpose or a direct result of this learning strategy; the comprehension and retention are.

36. A: The student has used procedural memory, that is, the type of memory for managing the application of grammatical rules to produce language. Having just learned the new English vocabulary word *focus,* she is additionally able to generate the past tense *focused* and the participle *focusing* because she has learned the English grammar rules for adding *–ed* to create past tense with regular verbs and *–ing* to create the progressive participle. Declarative (B) memory is the kind of memory that would enable her to recall previously learned vocabulary words, phrases, and sentences along with their meanings and other facts, knowledge, and concepts rather than to transform words grammatically by applying rules. Semantic (C) memory is the subtype of declarative memory used to remember vocabulary words, facts, and so on. Episodic (D) memory is the subtype of declarative memory used to remember personal experiences, events, and associated emotions.

37. C: This practice is culturally responsive and linguistically accessible because the Arab culture is the source of arithmetic and algebra, and the Arabic language is the origin of many arithmetic concepts and algebraic terms. It is also appropriate to the student's content-area abilities because the student displays a particular aptitude for arithmetic and algebra. Incorporating Arabic into

lessons as well as assignments can also inform other students about the origins of arithmetic, algebra, and their concepts and terminology. Therefore (A), (B), and (D) are all incorrect.

38. B: This is the only choice that directly uses multicultural human resources, that is, the English language learner (ELL) student's parent. The parent's presentation provides content-area learning in social studies and world history; the writing assignment facilitates English language development (ELD). Choice (A) uses realia for content-area learning, and the writing assignment facilitates ELD, but the teacher has not used human resources directly. Choice (C) facilitates ELD by presenting a vocabulary lesson but no content-area learning, and the teacher has used other modalities and multimedia, not human resources. Choice (D) promotes content-area learning and may also promote ELD for the ELL students as the teacher is presenting the math concepts in English; however, the teacher uses manipulatives rather than human resources for content-area learning in math concepts.

39. C: English language learner (ELL) students having intellectual disabilities and specific learning disabilities will have different cognitive needs than ELL students without these cognitive disabilities. Being in the same class, these students will not necessarily have different academic (A) needs as they will all be held to the same academic standards and benchmarks regardless of how their teacher helps them to meet these. Even if their L1s and English language proficiency (ELP) levels differ, all of their linguistic (B) needs are still to develop grade-level ELP. Not enough information is provided to know whether their cultural (D) needs differ; however, the information given clearly identifies differing cognitive needs for several students.

40. A: Edusoft's parent company is Educational Testing Service (ETS), publisher of the Test of English as a Foreign Language (TOEFL) and Test of English for International Communication (TOEIC) as well as Graduate Record Examinations (GRE), Praxis Series, and so on. On its comprehensive, interactive e-learning platform, English Discoveries Online (EDO), Edusoft offers a number of digital products, including a set of English for Specific Purposes (ESP) courses. These include Medical English, which would be of most use to the student preparing for a medical career. Pearson Education's English Language Learning Instruction (ELLIS) (B) is a digital learning program for teachers. Instant Immersion offers interactive programs in different languages. The advanced English language learner (ELL) student would probably not need these, and they have no specialized medical language. Lane's English as a Second Language (ESL) (D) is a valuable, free e-book including vocabulary, parts of speech, social expressions, handwriting, numbers, and review passages and dialogues focusing on basic ESL; the advanced English language proficiency (ELP) student would not need it, and it does not offer a specialized medical English course.

41. D: In a longitudinal study of electronic teacher feedback provided to English language learner (ELL) students, researchers found it equally explicit and systematic (A) as handwritten feedback; equally effective at evoking student revisions (B) to improve content, organization, grammatical structure, and surface characteristics; and equally based on student needs (C). Hence, electronic feedback was found neither inferior nor superior to handwritten feedback but similar and equally effective. The authors concluded that electronic feedback should not be avoided.

42. A: Emergent literacy theory assumes that developmental pre-reading and prewriting skills and behaviors like phonological awareness, language, conceptual knowledge, and letter knowledge can be taught. Interactive literacy theory (A) assumes that readers utilize knowledge at word, syntactic, and all other levels, including word decoding and interpretive inferences and predictions; move reciprocally between parts and whole; and synthesize sensory and intellectual components in reading for comprehension. The funds of knowledge theory (C) assumes that a student's home or

community cognitive and cultural resources can inform classroom learning. Because (A) is correct, (D) is incorrect.

43. C: Researchers studying teenage English language learner (ELL) students who were refugees and consequently had limited or no literacy in their own languages or English found that evidence-based instructional approaches for teaching academic English literacy to ELL students, such as the Mutually Adaptive Learning Paradigm MALP (A), the Cognitive Academic Language Learning Approach CALLA (B), or the Sheltered Instruction Observation Protocol (SIOP) (D), while effective for other ELL students, were insufficient for students lacking literacy in either language. Instead, they found that an equally evidence-based approach of guided reading and keeping running records as the foundation and framework for developing English-language print literacy was more effective for multidimensional literacy instruction addressing continua in both content and context.

44. C: Within the English language proficiency (ELP) levels of emerging, expanding, and bridging, California designates the relative amount of scaffolding educators probably need to provide students to enable them to meet the state's English language development (ELD) standards. Hence, a student at any one of the three proficiency levels could need any one of these support levels. Therefore, each support level does not correspond respectively to each proficiency level (A). The support levels are not entirely separate from the Proficiency Level Descriptors (PLDs) (B). These support levels do not explain how to differentiate instruction and provide support (D) at each proficiency level; they only indicate how much scaffolding a student is expected to need within that student's identified proficiency level.

45. B: English language development (ELD) standards in California are designed to help English language learner (ELL) students develop their English language skills to the point that they will eventually attain the state's English language arts (ELA) standards. The ELD standards also are designed to enable teachers to assess ELL students' progress toward meeting the ELA standards. Hence, if ELL students meet the ultimate goal of satisfying the ELA standards for all students in the state, they will automatically have met the ELD standards in the process. Thus, it is not true that ELL students attaining ELD standards will not achieve ELA standards (A). It is a misrepresentation to say that the two are strictly sequential or consecutive (C): ELL students are not restricted to meeting ELD standards before attempting ELA standards; as ELD standards-based instruction helps them develop their EL skills, they are concurrently progressing toward meeting the ELA standards. Neither are the two mutually exclusive (D) but interrelated.

46. D: The question describes a composition intended to convince or persuade its audience to take a certain position—that one candidate is a better choice—and then to act upon it by voting for that candidate. A narrative (A) composition would tell a story to an audience wanting to read or hear about events or experiences for the purpose of exploring and understanding a character, teaching a life lesson, sharing one's experience with others, or entertaining rather than persuading. An expository (B) composition would present facts and information to an audience seeking these for the purpose of educating or informing rather than persuading. A descriptive (C) composition would use sensory imagery and specific details to depict a scene, place or time, event, or experience for the purpose of enabling readers or listeners to feel as though they were actually experiencing it themselves, rather than persuading them of anything, to share an experience as realistically as if they had been there.

47. D: Each of these three error types occurs once: An error of verb tense (A) occurs with "had ... went," which should be *had ... gone* for the past perfect tense. An error of number (B) occurs with "By the times," plural, which should be *By the time,* singular. An error of agreement (C) occurs

between the present tense "I get there" and the past perfect tense "had . . . [gone]": This must be either "By the time I get there they *have* already gone," present tense, or "By the time I *got* there they had already gone," past and past perfect tenses, for the verbs in the sentence to agree.

48. B: The most complex tasks will not necessarily always require the most scaffolding (A), for example, when they are given to students whose cognitive, academic, and English language proficiency (ELP) levels match this complexity. Students with the lowest ELP levels will not necessarily always need the most scaffolding (C), for example, when the task is commensurate with their cognitive, academic, and ELP levels. Students with the highest ELP levels will not necessarily always need the least scaffolding (D), for example, if a student with higher ELP is still below grade level academically.

49. A: Videos are visual, auditory, and graphic and can use real people in real-life situations as well as multiple modalities; they can physically, concretely illustrate abstract concepts. Accompanying videos with verbs describing what people are doing and accompanying actions performed in the present, past, and future with corresponding verb tenses would make an effective strategy for creating background knowledge of verb conjugation. Rote memorization (B) is not advisable for students who have no idea of the abstract concept behind the words; they will not understand what they are trying to memorize. Rote tasks with words devoid of relevant context make it difficult for students to retain or apply them correctly. Similarly, fill-in-the-blank worksheets of sentences with verbs omitted (C) would be ineffective because English language learner (ELL) students with no formal grammar instruction in their L1s will not be able to deduce the correct verb tenses from sentence context alone without learning the grammatical paradigms first: They have no frame of reference. Translations (D) will not help because these students never learned about conjugating verbs in their native languages.

50. C: Based on the description, these are primarily student–student interactions as they involve peer tutoring. While the tutoring could involve reading a text (A), the description does not say this; they could just as well be tutoring peers in English listening or speaking skills or practicing English writing skills. The teacher's only role described here was assigning the students to pairs. If the pairs then work independently with minimal teacher guidance, it is not primarily a teacher–student (B) interaction. Because (C) is correct, (D) is incorrect.

51. C: When planning Specially Designed Academic Instruction in English (SDAIE) lessons for English language learner (ELL) students in content-area subjects, teachers should find ways to integrate all language skills—listening, speaking, reading, and writing—into instruction across the curriculum. Therefore, the most effective use of SDAIE lessons would be to assign reading tasks, writing tasks, oral presentations as speaking tasks, and discussions as listening and speaking tasks, not only in English language development (ELD) classes but also in math, science, social studies, and other content subjects. Choices (A) and (B) do not integrate all four domains—listening, speaking, reading, and writing—across the curriculum but limit instruction to only two of those in one or two subjects. Choice (D) omits listening and speaking tasks entirely across the curriculum. Waiting for students to reach higher oral English language proficiency (ELP) levels is ineffective without providing instructional listening and speaking tasks to enable them to attain those levels.

52. B: The most appropriate teacher strategy for this student would be to select from among multiple strategies according to which is best for each subject; for example, when the student's reading and writing English language proficiency (ELP) levels permit the student to perform up to his or her subject ability levels, written assessments could be used, but all written assessments (D) should not be used considering the student's writing ELP level is much lower than speaking and

listening ELP levels. Authentic assessments should be an option when the student's ELP levels prevent performing fully in some subjects, but these should not be the only assessments used (A). The teacher should scaffold any assessment tasks as needed but not necessarily all (C) if the student does not need it in some subjects or with some forms of assessment.

53. C: In a Specially Designed Academic Instruction in English (SDAIE) lesson, if the teacher assigns activities for the students that apply the subject's key concepts and vocabulary, and these activities also utilize materials or resources that do the same, the students will experience the lesson's most important ideas and terminology within a context that makes these meaningful to them as they engage in an activity. Providing the ideas and terms in sentence contexts (A), assigning students to use the ideas and words in sentences (B), and giving students glossaries with translations (D), are useful for teaching vocabulary definitions but will not contextualize important concepts and terminology in any authentic activities wherein students can experience their applications.

54. C: The best strategy of the choices offered for scaffolding a Specially Designed Academic Instruction in English (SDAIE) lesson's accompanying assignment, especially for a hands-on activity, is to demonstrate the assignment instructions to provide a model for English language learner (ELL) students to follow in completing the assignment. Teacher demonstration provides authentic modeling and eliminates or overcomes language barriers. Printed (A) or oral (B) instructions in English, or both of these together (D), do neither of these.

55. A: Debriefing is a cognitive or metacognitive strategy wherein the teacher helps English language learners (ELLs) develop more autonomy in learning by guiding them carefully to reflect on what and how they learned and to use metacognition to analyze the cognitive processes they used in performing learning tasks. Hence, debriefing involves reflection. However, reflection does not necessarily always involve debriefing (B). Students may reflect on their learning independently or as assigned by their teacher but without the guidance of debriefing. Another metacognitive strategy teachers can instruct students in explicitly is to use text features; however, debriefing does not require this (C). Debriefing is not equal to self-evaluation (D): In self-evaluation, for example, students might complete a teacher-made checklist showing which learning tasks they accomplished, rating how well they did them, and so on.

56. C: The best way for teachers to communicate to English language learner (ELL) students what they expect of their performance in English language development (ELD) and content-area subjects is to provide them with clear models of the outcomes they should become able to achieve. Modeling both surmounts language barriers and provides authentic demonstration; written English does neither (A), and written L1 (B) does the former but not the latter. A pretest and then a post-test (D) will establish what students knew and could do before the instruction and what they know and can do after the instruction, but they will not communicate to students before or during instruction what they will be expected to know or be able to do.

57. C: English language learner (ELL) students should have text analysis and interpretation assignments as part of Specially Designed Academic Instruction in English (SDAIE) lessons in both written and oral form to develop the listening, speaking, and writing as well as reading domains of English language development (ELD). Therefore, these assignments should not be limited to writing (A) or listening and speaking (B). Individual oral exams with the teacher (D) with the excuse of avoiding student embarrassment will deprive them of the experience and practice they need with using conversational and academic English to listen and speak, that is, communicate, with their peers as well as their teachers.

58. D: To assess whether English language learner (ELL) students have achieved the content in Specially Designed Academic Instruction in English (SDAIE) lessons, teachers should best use not only oral (A) or only written (B) assessments, as some ELL students will perform better in one and some in the other, and not only oral and written (C) verbal assessments, but these plus nonverbal assessments. Receptive language acquisition precedes and exceeds expressive language acquisition, so ELL students often comprehend the English-language content they have heard and read better than they can express in speech and writing. Hence, they also should be given nonverbal assessments to obtain the most accurate demonstration of what they have learned.

59. D: Hands-on activities (A) give English language learner (ELL) students authentic contexts for students to learn subject-area content while also developing their English language skills. Guarded vocabulary (B) simplifies English language to enable ELL students to connect new subject content to their first languages and prior experiences. Cooperative learning (C) enhances two-way communication with peers for academic learning purposes.

60. B: Generation 1.5 English language learner (ELL) students were native to other countries and languages, beginning American educations around 12 years old. Thus, their cultural values and family relationships are more likely to conflict with the cultures and values of American higher education institutions and workplaces. Under-schooled ELL students (A) have either missed a great deal of school or had extremely poor educations but may have come to America at any age. For example, children of migrant workers could have been in the United States all or most of their lives and yet missed a lot of school; other children arrived younger but missed several school years or grades before enrollment here, and so on. Long-term ELL students (C) have not developed English language skills adequate for academic progress but were born in the United States to immigrant parents. Under-schooled ELLs can have longer-term exposure to American culture; long-term ELLs, regardless of cultural traditions within families and communities, have been exposed to American culture all their lives. Hence, these two groups are less likely to experience cultural conflicts in America related to college and work than Generation 1.5 ELLs.

CTEL 3

1. C: Nonverbal communication patterns are examples of internal elements of culture. Arts and literature are external, not internal elements (A) of culture. Traditional rituals and rites are internal, not external (B) elements of culture. Social roles and status are internal, not external (D) elements of culture. Other internal cultural elements include customs, beliefs, values, mores, expectations, family structures, gender roles, and work and leisure patterns. Other external cultural elements include government, religious structures, language, technology, food, shelter, and clothing.

2. D: Cultural relativism, (B) and (D), is the perspective that characteristics of particular elements of a culture, for example, language, are differentially determined by features of that culture. For example, linguist Benjamin Whorf hypothesized that geographical features of a certain environment influenced the lexicon of the people living there, citing as evidence that Eskimo languages had more than 20 different words for snow, whereas other languages had only one. Thus, cultural relativism is exclusive. Ethnocentrism, (C) and (D), is the perspective of being oriented exclusively toward one's own culture, perceiving everything in terms of that culture, and ignoring, rejecting, or judging other cultures in comparison to one's own. Cultural congruence, (A) and (C), is the perspective of acknowledging and accommodating diverse cultural backgrounds in education, health care, and so on, by making these services culturally responsive and compatible. Hence, cultural congruence is inclusive. Cultural pluralism (A) acknowledges multiple and diverse cultural traditions and

influences and is also inclusive. Cultural universals (B) are elements found in and across all cultures despite their diversity and thus are inclusive.

3. B: The zone of proximal development (ZPD) describes what a student can do with assistance that he or she cannot yet do independently and, moreover, that what the student can do with assistance now predicts what he or she will be able to do independently in the future. Therefore, it considers not only the student's current language proficiency level (A) or past history of language development (C), and not just what the student can do only with help (D), but also that what the student can do today with help, he or she will be able to do without it in the future.

4. C: Research studies with English language learner (ELL) students find that low-income ELLs tend to have less formal education; both factors influence academic achievement. Low-income, low-education ELLs are found to be behind their peers in academic readiness and language skills and more in need of culturally responsive, research evidence-based instruction. Because income largely determines education in ELLs, (A) and (B) are both incorrect. Because income and education both affect ELL school performance, (D) is also incorrect.

5. D: Allport deemed in-groups "psychologically primary." He said that "love prejudice is far more basic to human life than . . . hate prejudice." Hence, (C) is incorrect regarding his position. He pointed out that people defend their own and their group's values "at the expenses of other people's interests or safety." Thus, he found that "hate prejudice springs from a reciprocal love prejudice underneath." Therefore, he felt both that favoritism for in-groups took precedence over aversion for out-groups (A) and that the former was the reason for the latter (B).

6. A: This is an example of assimilation, which involves merging into the new culture more than preserving one's native culture. Choice (B) is an example of biculturalism. Choice (C) is an example of acculturation. Choice (D) is an example of accommodation.

7. D: These students are likely all experiencing culture shock, having just been displaced from their native countries, cultures, languages, homes, and schools. Culture shock is described as having four stages: First is the honeymoon or euphoric stage, wherein the student is excited about the new environment and having a wonderful time (A) learning all about everything. The shock stage is when students realize the extent of cultural differences between their native and new countries and cultures and feel overwhelmed by the surroundings and verbal and social signals they cannot understand. Students in culture shock may seem withdrawn, silent, passive and isolated (B), or they may act out their frustration aggressively in the classroom (C). The third and fourth stages are (3) integration and (4) acceptance.

8. D: An English language learner (ELL) student who attended more school prior immigrating has both the advantages of being accustomed to the idea and practice of formal education and potentially being more informed through education about national, cultural, and linguistic differences; this student may also have the disadvantage in many cases of having to adjust to an educational system very different from their native ones. A student's country or culture of origin (A) can be more conducive or prohibitive to acculturation depending on its relative similarity or difference to America. A family's reasons for immigrating (B) can encourage or discourage acculturation depending whether they immigrated voluntarily, for example, for better educational and employment opportunities, more political or religious freedoms, and so on, or involuntarily, in which case they may be less likely to adjust. A student's age upon arrival (C) is usually more conducive to acculturation when younger and less when older. (Exceptions can include teens capable of independent choices who embrace the new culture. However, children exposed to new

culture very young have little or no memory of native culture unless their families maintain its practices at home, and even then, they still constantly experience the new culture outside home.)

9. B: Avoidant, (A) and (D), conflict style denies the problem by repressing feelings and thoughts or walking away from it. Limitations are that it may never resolve the problem; emotions can erupt afterward. Uses are when confrontation appears threatening or one needs additional time for preparation. Confronting, (A) and (B), style gets what one wants regardless of expense to others and involves taking over, interrupting, disregarding others' feelings and opinions, raising one's voice, and physical violence at times. Limitations are evoking defensiveness, inhibiting others' self-expression, and exacerbating conflicts. Uses are when action is required immediately or one sees no other options. Compromising (B) style allows each party to win and lose some things and demonstrates motivation to discuss and solve problems. Limitations are resolving an immediate conflict, but not a larger, underlying problem, and both parties' ending up dissatisfied. Uses are when a decision is needed quickly about a minor issue or nothing else works. Problem-solving (D) style involves directly expressing needs, desires, and feelings; closely examining conflict sources; and finding a solution to please everybody. Limitations are requiring good communication skills and time. Use is moving stubborn others toward problem resolution.

10. A: This exercise helps students to develop empathy by temporarily, walking in another's shoes, and to explore stereotypes many hold about various groups. By placing themselves into a different identity and then considering how their lives might change, how others will treat them, and so on, students are given an opportunity to experience how other people may feel, developing empathy, and to realize how people often hold ideas, images, or beliefs about whole groups that are not applicable to every individual within each group.

11. A: California has the most immigrants of any state in the United States—more than 10 million, equaling one in four nationally and 27% of California's population as of 2011. The Department of Homeland Security reported that only 27% of immigrants in California were undocumented (B); 47% were naturalized citizens, and 26% had visas, green cards, or other legal entry. While the majority (53%) of immigrants in California is Latin American, from 2007 to 2011, the majority was Asian (C). Asians make up 37% of California's immigrants. From 2007 to 2011, 53% of immigrants were from Asia, while 31% were from Latin America. Hence Asians were the majority of immigrants from 2007 to 2011, but they are not the majority (D): Latin Americans still comprise more of the population.

12. D: In 2012, Los Angeles County received 2,175,200 legal immigrants according to the California state Department of Finance. That year, Orange County received 534,509 legal immigrants. San Francisco County (A) received 286,652 legal immigrants in 2012. Santa Clara County (C) received 480,753. San Diego County (C) received 438,624. Therefore, with Los Angeles County being first, the second-most legal immigrants to California in 2012 came to Orange County, the third most to Santa Clara County, the fourth most to San Diego County, and the fifth most to San Francisco County.

13. B: When workers immigrate to America seeking better wages, this is an example of a pull factor: They are attracted to potentially better situations. Refugees from wars in other countries (A) are experiencing a push factor: They are ejected from their native countries. So are those escaping terrorist political regimes (C) in their homelands. While they may choose to flee rather than being sent away, they usually feel they have no other choice and thus are forced (pushed) to leave. Those exiled for political or religious reasons by governments in other countries (D) are also experiencing a push factor.

14. C: When assessing students in an L2, they will often not perform in the L2 up to the norms in their L1s (A). Cultural differences often do influence child–adult interactions during L2 assessment (B). Because of these factors, there is a risk that students will be over-identified as having developmental disorders or delays when tested in their second language (C), more than a risk of their being under-identified (D).

15. A: Assessment should never be limited to a single instrument. Using multiple and varied types of assessments is always advocated for obtaining the most accurate and comprehensive picture of the student's abilities. Experts do recommend considering how long an English language learner (ELL) child has been learning English (B), the child's language abilities in his or her L1 (D), and the child's language abilities in English (C). Standardized instruments are available to help educators estimate the probabilities that an ELL child has a language-learning problem using the aforementioned considerations and test results.

16. D: By designating four types of physical distance between or among people during interactions, Hall created a system for observing how distance affects communication, including the fact that it varies among different cultures. Intimate space, used for whispering, touching, or embracing, is closer than personal space, used for interactions among family members or close friends; personal space is closer than social space, used for interactions among acquaintances. Social space is closer than public space, used for public speaking. Thus, personal and social space are not equal (A); neither are social and public space (B). The effects of distance on communication are not the same among cultures (C) but vary culturally.

17. D: None of these is universal across cultures. For example, in some Muslim cultures, touching (A) between opposite sexes is strictly prohibited, excepting married couples, and even then still prohibited in public. Certain hand gestures (B) have completely different meanings in different cultures. For example, visiting Australia, President George W. Bush attempted to wave a peace sign (two fingers making a V), but his palm faced in, not out; in Australia, this signaled the audience to go @#$% themselves. Thumbs-up means OK or good in America and Europe, but is offensive in Asian and Muslim countries. A raised hand, palm out, means stop in England and America, but in Malaysia and Singapore, it is used to ask permission to speak, to hail, or to get somebody's attention. The corona (index and pinky fingers raised) variously means rock and roll, the Longhorn mascot at the University of Texas, the devil, the *Karana Mudra* for dispelling evil in Buddhist and Hindu cultures, or a cuckold in the Mediterranean. Eye contact (C) is valued as showing attention or interest in America but is disrespectful for women in Japan.

18. A: American culture is considered low context and analytical; Asian cultures are considered high context and holistic. Low-context cultures find meaning more important than context and individual speakers responsible for making messages understood. They compartmentalize areas of life, value explicit and verbal communication, prefer showing initiative and making decisions independently, and can work together without knowing a lot of information about others. High-context cultures find context, that is, nonverbal communication, more important and listeners responsible for understanding messages. They regard life holistically: Areas of life are not separated; neither are speakers from messages. They prefer implicit, indirect, and nonverbal communication; prefer building long-term, trusting, deep relationships and making consensus decisions; and need a lot of information about others to work together.

19. C: An effective strategy for intercultural interactions is to keep an open mind for accepting new information that is not familiar about a culture or cultural group. It is a common human

ethnocentric habit to disregard or distort information that does not fit into existing worldviews. Another effective strategy is not generalizing from one area of an individual's competence or incompetence to all other areas (A). For example, just because somebody speaks poor English does not indicate that he or she is generally incompetent. Rather than being honest about discomfort with people from other cultures (B), it is better to keep one's normal discomfort from making one treat those people differently. While acknowledging to oneself that some discomfort with people from unfamiliar cultures is natural, it is important not to treat them unfairly or with favoritism. It is not considerate or a way to avoid embarrassing others not to explain cultural expectations (D): People from other cultures cannot figure out our unwritten cultural rules, so one must expect having to explain these, even if it is embarrassing or uncomfortable.

20. B: When interacting with others, especially from different cultures, the first interpretation of their behavior is not necessarily accurate. For example, suppose an individual from another culture was avoiding eye contact during a discussion. An American might assume he or she was bored, uncomfortable, angry, and so on, because Americans view eye contact as a sign of attention and interest; but not all other cultures do. To check assumptions, one can give specific feedback about observable behaviors, for example, "I noticed you were not making eye contact during our discussion." You can request clarification of your interpretations of these behaviors (C), for example, "Can you tell me what was happening or why you were not looking at me?" Alternatively, one could also provide feedback about one's own response (D), for example, "I felt like I was being ignored when you were not looking at me. Can you tell me what was happening?" Experts also advise a quasi-brainstorming process, of listing all possible interpretations for the other person's behavior.

21. D: Rather than explaining her rationale to parents (A), which assumes she will use the strategy, the teacher should first confirm or rule out whether this individual student actually does have the cultural trait about which the teacher has read. This also takes precedence over simply continuing to do more reading about the student's culture (B): Written materials, though valuable, may not give the same insights into as many dimensions of the culture as getting information directly from real students, parents, and community members from that culture. While coworkers could provide ideas for alternative strategies (C), the teacher still needs to find out the individual student's personal preferences first.

22. C: The teacher's cultural assumptions are typical of the American individualist culture, which values individual achievement and expression and competition to be the best. This differed from the student's cultural values, typical of a collectivist culture, which values group harmony and deferring individual needs for the common good. Hence, she initially did not understand why the English language learner (ELL) student excelled at teamwork and supporting teammates but made no effort individually to compete or win against classmates. If the teacher's instructional methods motivated teamwork more than competitiveness (A), she would have the same results with all students and not be puzzled by the ELL student's behaviors. The same applies if her teaching style were more effective with teams than individuals (D). While it is entirely possible that the rest of the class had more highly competitive than team-oriented students (B), the question states that the teacher finds an answer after inquiring about and researching the ELL student's culture, indicating cultural differences.

23. A: Informal conversations with the students themselves can help the teacher acquire in-depth knowledge about the individual students' cultural experiences. Observing the students' behaviors during interaction with classmates (B) could inform the teacher about how the students interact socially with peers but would not grant in-depth knowledge about the students' own cultural

experiences the way their actually telling the teacher about them would. Interviewing the students' parents (C) would inform the teacher about their cultures and the families' cultural practices but would not inform the teacher about the students' cultural experiences as directly as the students themselves could. Community resources (D) could inform the teacher about the students' cultures in general but not about individual students' cultural experiences.

24. B: Cooperative learning groups will be culturally congruent with the students' collectivist cultural backgrounds as they are accustomed to working together to achieve the welfare of the whole group. The students from African cultures with strong oral traditions and those from Latin American cultures that emphasize expressiveness can make the oral presentation for their groups instead of those from Asian cultures, who are less comfortable with individual presentations. Assigning all students to make individual oral presentations (A) would lack this advantage. Independent study projects (C) would not address these students' collectivist backgrounds but would emphasize individual achievement instead of group effort and would require oral presentations of all students, including those uncomfortable with these. A bowl-style knowledge contest (D) emphasizing competition over cooperation would not be culturally compatible for these students.

25. D: Teacher expectations should be uniformly high for both English language learner (ELL) and native English-speaking students. While teachers should provide culturally responsive instruction, linguistic accommodations, and English language development (ELD) or Specially Designed Academic Instruction in English (SDAIE) to enable ELL students to develop English language skills and to learn and succeed academically with subject content in English, this does not mean their expectations of ELL and native English-speaking students should differ.

26. C: To show respect for student linguistic diversity while facilitating their English language development (ELD) and content learning, teachers should teach ELD to English language learner (ELL) students and also allow and validate their natural L1 use. Not teaching English (A) will impede their school success here. Permitting only English use in school (B) denies their linguistic diversity. Telling parents to learn and speak only English at home (D) not only disrespects diversity, but moreover, it is out of bounds for teachers to tell parents what to do at home.

27. D: A school's learning environment would be most culturally inclusive when multicultural perspectives are incorporated into all subjects across the curriculum rather than only presenting such perspectives during social studies class (A) or on special culture days (B) or only having students examine them as enrichment projects (C). In a culturally inclusive learning environment, multicultural viewpoints permeate curriculum and instruction rather than being introduced only in isolated activities or classes.

28. B: Intergroup relations refer to relations between or among different groups. Intragroup relations refer to relations among members within the same group. Answer (A) has the definitions reversed. These two terms do not mean the same thing (C). Because (B) is correct, (D) is incorrect.

29. A. Setting up home or community visits is one way teachers can offer English language learner (ELL) parents tips and ways they can help their children with their reading, English language development (ELD), and homework. However, it is necessary for teachers first to ascertain if their union or school district allows such visits (B). Interpreters do not constitute intrusive third parties for ELL parents (C); they are often necessary and very helpful when parents speak little or no English. Experts advise teachers to respect the constraints and preferences of ELL families

regarding times and locations for visits; for example, parents may want or need to meet with teachers at community centers, at churches, or in their homes rather than on school grounds (D).

30. B: By employing a variety of learning activities, assignments, and teaching strategies according to the differing needs of diverse students, a teacher helps to establish an inclusive learning environment. Using a single teaching method with all students (A) will not address their different backgrounds, experiences, skills, and learning styles. Rather than devoting a single class to studying cultural diversity (C), teachers can teach more inclusively by integrating diversity throughout the entire curriculum. To teach inclusively, teachers can intentionally establish safer learning environments by setting and enforcing some ground rules for students rather than not having any (D).

31. D: One way to help involve English language learner (ELL) parents with their children's school is to contact other parents with similar socioeconomic and cultural profiles and recruit their help in furthering positive home–school communication. Parent liaisons can offer communication and instruction to other ELL families and community members. Another effective educator strategy is to be open to meeting with parents outside of normal school days (A) and locations to accommodate parental limitations with child care, transportation, and work schedules. Other cultures can have very different school systems, so educators often need to teach them about the collaborative, communicative style of American school cultures (B), or parents will feel unsure about how they can participate actively in children's educations at schools. Researchers also find educators must connect immigrant families with businesses and community programs to help meet their basic needs (C) before family school involvement can succeed.

32. C: Schools can provide training to diverse parents in effectively tutoring their children at home in math, reading, and other school subjects. It is also appropriate and important for schools to offer parent education about specific disabilities (A), which can help parents detect these in their children, recognize need for referral, or become informed about school and other services available for students with disabilities and about how to work with disabilities if their children have them. Prenatal care information is another area that should not only be left to Planned Parenthood (B); schools also can offer parent training classes with this information, which is often much needed and appreciated. Another area where schools can help is with information on free or reduced-cost aftercare opportunities (D), which are not only available from community agencies.

33. A: Educators can invite community members to their schools to share their backgrounds from different cultures and languages with their students and faculty. Teachers are not the only ones who can explain things about other languages (B); community members with diverse backgrounds often know about these and can share valuable information and insight. Expertise in content area subjects is also not confined to faculty (C); many community members are experts in particular content subjects and can share their knowledge with students, faculty, administrators, and other staff. Sharing information about various religious traditions (D) is not the same as requiring or teaching religion per se in public schools; it is acceptable and enriching to provide additional information about religions, just as it may also be included in school subjects like social studies.

34. D: School Governance Councils typically include students, parents, and community members as well as school personnel. Typically, these members are involved in conducting needs analyses for the school (A); analyzing the school's student achievement data (B); and developing, reviewing, revising, and approving school improvement plans (C) and advising school principals before submitting school improvement or accountability plans to the school superintendent.

35. C: The peaceable classroom program model (A) uses classroom conflict resolution as a classroom management technique. The curriculum infusion program (B) model teaches conflict management concepts by incorporating them into subject area content. The school mediation program (D) model uses mediation by a neutral third party as the main process of conflict resolution in schools, including peer mediation programs; trained, independent student mediator cadre programs; curriculum-linked mediation; community-linked, service learning mediation; truancy mediation; and special education mediation. The peaceable school program (C) model is also called the comprehensive conflict management program model. It encompasses curriculum infusion, classroom management, and mediation as well as training the whole school community to know and apply conflict management concepts and skills throughout daily school functions.

36. A: The contributions approach (C) involves including activities and texts about heroes, special events, and holidays from different cultural backgrounds without requiring these in the curriculum. For example, studying Thanksgiving traditions could include reading texts about historical Native American contributions to the formation of the Thanksgiving holiday. The additive approach (A) incorporates literature and other content, perspectives, themes, and concepts from diverse cultures into the curriculum without restructuring it. For example, studying Thanksgiving could include viewing it from the Native American perspective. The transformation approach (D) restructures the curriculum to make diversity a fundamental and integral component. For example, studying Thanksgiving could involve a whole unit wherein students apply critical thinking skills to explore cultural conflict. The social action approach (B) not only transforms curriculum but, moreover, involves students in attempting to effect social change. For example, studying Thanksgiving could include interacting with, learning from, and providing support to Native American community members.

37. B: When transforming to multicultural curriculum, a major change in content involves teaching the works of underrepresented peoples. For example, economics courses have traditionally covered only Western economic systems, but to be multicultural, they must include worldwide economic systems. Histories of oppression cannot be confined only to history classes (A) but must be taught across the curriculum. For example, in science, teaching about X-ray technology can include reasons for the discrepancy with who is credited with inventing it versus who actually did invent it. In literature, the small proportion of female authors and their use of male pen names can be included. Just as educators do not expect students to comprehend concepts in math and science from a single example, they also must illustrate multicultural concepts with multiple examples (C) to effect comprehensive curriculum content changes. In teaching about the countries of origin and lives of the underrepresented and oppressed, they must be represented as normal people rather than unusual (D), exotic, or extinct.

38. D: A teacher who has visited a country some students come from should not only use this experience to inform general instruction (A) but also share his or her personal experience (B) of that country with students; they should invite the students from that country to share their own personal perspectives (C) about the country. This makes instruction inclusive of global perspectives as well as making it locally responsive by grounding it in both faculty and student autobiographical contexts.

39. B: Students from collectivist cultures, where group harmony and interdependence are valued more, are less inclined to want to express themselves (A) than students from individualist cultures like America's, where individual expression is valued more. Students from collectivist cultures may avoid drawing attention to themselves, defer to the teacher's authority more, and be less likely to volunteer information in classes (B). Collectivist cultures emphasize cooperation above

competition, so students from these backgrounds are more likely to help others (C) rather than wanting to compete with and best them by getting better grades (D). (Note: This does not necessarily apply to students from Asian American families, or from Americanized Asian urban centers, who are often extremely achievement driven regarding high grades. However, even these students usually do not focus on getting better grades than other students but rather on personally getting the highest grades possible, for example, how close to 100% their GPAs are in each class and overall.)

40. C: The teacher can best help access prior knowledge to facilitate the assignment by having the student dictate a story orally using a provided recorder and then transcribing the dictation. The rich oral tradition of the student's culture facilitates storytelling, and as speaking English typically precedes writing English for most English language learners (ELLs), the student can more easily transcribe spoken English into written English. Giving written translations (A) overlooks the student's oral tradition by providing only written materials in both languages. Telling the student to write in L1 and then translate it into L2 (B) also disregards speech in favor of writing. Telling the student to use an earlier L1 composition as a guide (D) is less appropriate because, if the student's native culture has a strong oral tradition, the student may not have had formal instruction in written language and may not have an earlier composition in the L1. Even if he or she does, it may be no help as a guide as it is not in English and may otherwise be too different from the current assignment.